Training Guide for Heaven

Running for the Prize

DAVID L. JOHNSON *and*
RICHARD A. HANSEN

WESTBOW
PRESS®
A DIVISION OF THOMAS NELSON
& ZONDERVAN

WestBow Press books may be ordered through booksellers or by contacting:

WestBow Press
A Division of Thomas Nelson & Zondervan
1663 Liberty Drive
Bloomington, IN 47403
www.westbowpress.com
844-714-3454

ISBN: 978-1-6642-1771-3 (sc)
ISBN: 978-1-6642-1772-0 (hc)
ISBN: 978-1-6642-1885-7 (e)

Library of Congress Control Number: 2021900400

Print information available on the last page.

WestBow Press rev. date: 03/10/2021

Contents

Acknowledgments

Several people read drafts of this book. We are very grateful for the feedback on the manuscript from Ken Clinton, Bob and Donna Ericson, Herb Froemming, Bruce and Vicki Hagberg, Pat Hansen (Rick's wife), Sam Houston, Toni Jasinski, Barbie Korngable, Al and Sandy Kretsinger, Rylee Mitchell-Nodine, Bruce Peterson, and JoAnn Foster Swanson.

The Lord bless you and keep you; the Lord make his face shine on you and be gracious to you; the Lord turn his face toward you and give you peace.

—Numbers 6:24–26

Introduction

Have you ever gazed at the stars in the night sky and wondered why you are here and what happens after you die? The two questions are interrelated, you know.

What happens to you after you die dictates your purpose in life, why you are here. The Bible answers both questions. Our time on earth is a relatively short training period for our life after death.

Life on earth is not all there is, and life after death is not some fanciful wish. The Bible is clear about this. There is a heaven. There is only one way to get to heaven. Plus, there are crowns and rewards promised once we get there.

As adults, we hadn't heard much about heaven, crowns, or rewards, so we decided to research the topic. The result is this book, which also includes a short primer about Christianity. The source of this research, the Bible, is the most well-attested ancient book in existence. God doesn't expect us to blindly believe what the Bible says. There is good evidence all around us that it is true.

We will provide that evidence and explain what the Bible says about our eternal destination. We will explain what is known about heaven, the prophetic timeline about future events, rewards available to us in heaven, how to earn those rewards on earth, and how to keep our eyes on the prize by standing on the promises of God.

These are confusing times, especially with viruses spreading around the world causing disease, such as COVID-19. Nothing is more important than knowing the truth and how to apply that truth to your life. Nothing is more important than planning for life after death. You'd better be ready; life after death is forever, and there are only two destinations.

1

The Most Important
Question in Your Life

Life is a journey. There is a beginning: you are born. For many people, there is a middle: you go to school, work, get married, have children, reach middle age, and retire. There is an end: you die.

So what happens at the end when you die? Is it really an end? A transition to something else? Shouldn't you know? Is it even knowable?

Yes, it is knowable, and yes, you should know. What happens when you die is the most important question in your life. Yet few people want to think about it.

We all know for certain that life here on earth has an end. Everyone dies. The mortality rate is 100 percent, but is it truly the end? Could the end be merely the starting point for something bigger? Much, much bigger? The Bible says yes!

The decisions you make in this life, the way you live on this earth, affects what will happen to you when this life on earth ends. It profoundly affects your destination. There are many forks in the road as we proceed on life's journey. Death is the final fork in the road, with only two branches. We are offered a choice of which branch to take and must make that decision before we die.

So, the most important question in your life is: what happens to you when you die? The object of life, then, should be to arrive at a desired destination when life ends. All journeys start with a destination in mind. You work backward from the destination to figure out how to get there.

Goals

Let's say you plan to drive to the Wisconsin Dells from Minneapolis for a family vacation. What would you do? You'd find Wisconsin Dells on the map and trace your finger back to Minneapolis. You'd see that Interstate Highway 90 takes you from Minneapolis to Wisconsin Dells. It will take around three and a half hours to get there. About one tank of gasoline will do.

You'd research what there is to do at Wisconsin Dells. What are the attractions? There are Duck Boats, waterslides, go-karts, and more. You'd determine what clothes to bring. You'd make a reservation at a hotel. You'd decide when to leave Minneapolis to arrive at your destination, what to do once you get there, and what to bring.

You have a goal, Wisconsin Dells. You make a commitment, marking it on your calendar, or if you work, arranging with the boss to take the time off. Assuming you have a family, your spouse and children are all anticipating the trip. Barring some unforeseen circumstances, your destination is assured.

You are clear in your mind why you have this goal. It's your vacation. It's time off from work. It's a reward, and it will be fun. You anticipate the joy it will bring to your family.

If you should encounter rain on your trip, will you turn back? It is an obstacle. Of course not; you won't turn back. You have a goal. You are committed to the goal. You understand why you need to achieve that goal. Therefore, you will push on.

To train for something, you need a specific and concrete goal. You need to fully understand why that goal is important. The *why* will allow you to overcome obstacles. You won't persist to the end unless you clearly understand why you need to accomplish that goal.

Let's use another example. You want to run a 5K during the summer. The destination is the finish line. Why do you want to finish? Maybe you need the exercise to lose weight and look better. Maybe you want to lower your blood pressure to avoid medications and save money on future health care. Maybe you want to feel the exultation of completing something you've never done before or something you can accomplish all on your own.

It is essential you clearly understand why this goal is important so you can put in the miles training. There are going to be some days you don't want to run, but if you remind yourself of the *why*, you can push yourself forward. If you keep the reward in mind and visualize the feeling of crossing the finish line, you will lace up those shoes and go run when you would rather sit on the couch and watch TV.

If you fail to plan, plan to fail. You need to work backward and create a training schedule. How many months until the race? Let's say it is two months. Maybe you start out running half a mile a day, four days a week, and increase the mileage by a half mile each week until you reach four miles. If you do this, by the day of the race, you will have adequately prepared to reach your goal.

SMART Goals

In this book, we will use the popular SMART goals acronym:

- Specific: clear and unambiguous
- Measurable: can measure your progress
- Achievable: attainable and not impossible
- Realistic: within reach within the time specified
- Timely: includes a starting date and a target date

Using our 5K example, here is our SMART goal: I plan to run a 5K without stopping on July 31 and will begin training on June 1 by running half a mile each day without stopping, four days a week, and increasing the distance by half a mile each week until I can run four miles without stopping by race day.

This is a SMART goal because it is:

- Specific: clear and unambiguous. *Run four miles without stopping by July 31.*
- Measurable: can measure your progress. *Progress is measured in miles run.*
- Achievable: attainable and not impossible. *I can run half a mile now without stopping and can reach four miles without stopping in two months.*
- Realistic: within reach within the time specified. *Two months is doable, considering my age and fitness level.*
- Timely: includes a starting date and a target date. *I will start training June 1 and finish by July 31.*

We've just reviewed the minimum plans you would make to reach a vacation goal or a training goal. Doesn't it make sense to do this for the most important goal in your life, your destination at death? Does it make sense to plan more for a vacation or a 5K run than for your destination at death? No. It doesn't make sense! In fact, it is absurd. Talk about being penny wise and pound foolish.

What We Cover in This Book

The title of this book is *Training Guide for Heaven: Running for the Prize*. The apostle Paul in 1 Corinthians 9:24–27 writes:

> Do you not know that in a race all the runners run, but only one gets the prize? Run in such a way as to get the prize. Everyone who competes in the games goes into strict training. They do it to get a crown that will not last, but we do it to get a crown that will last forever. Therefore I do not run like someone running aimlessly; I do not fight like a boxer beating the air. No, I strike a blow to my body and make it my slave so that after I have preached to others, I myself will not be disqualified for the prize.

What is the prize Paul is talking about? He calls it a crown. He will receive it in heaven. Heaven is Paul's destination, and receiving a crown is his goal. It should be yours as well.

In chapter 2, we'll discuss what happens when you die. There are many different explanations that exist. We'll tell you the truth. Plus, we don't expect you to just take our word for it. We'll give you the evidence you need. You don't need blind faith. If you are going to believe in something, it better be true! After all, everything is at stake.

Can we have a concrete image of our goal—heaven? Yes, in chapter 3, we'll discuss what it's like and what you can do in heaven.

Can we pick our destination? Yes. We'll explain how in chapter 4.

Can we arrange for a departure date? No, but there are some future events we need to explain in chapter 5.

What are we training for? We are pointing ourselves toward heaven and training to receive rewards once we get there. In chapter 6, we'll discuss the crowns and rewards we can earn on earth and receive in heaven by living our life in a manner pleasing to God.

We will explain how to earn those rewards in chapter 7. That's the training guide part of the book. We spend all the time in the previous chapters to make sure that you fully understand why this goal is important and why it is real.

Finally, in chapter 8, we'll discuss how to stand on the promises of God when times get tough and training gets hard. In life, there are disappointments, frustrations, hardships, and many obstacles to overcome. We need to keep our goal in mind when the training gets tough.

2

Where Do We Go When We Die?

So where do we go when we die? What is our final destination? This is the most important question you can ask.

If we don't have a destination in mind, we can't formulate a concrete goal and prepare to get there. We will go through life haphazardly, without a purpose. A life without a purpose is empty and pointless.

You may think that your purpose is to get married and start a family. This is certainly a noble purpose, one of the most important in life. Children are a gift from God to be cherished. You may think your purpose in life is to get a job and pursue a career. Again, this is an important purpose, but there is a higher purpose in life, one more important than starting a family, raising children, or working.

Ecclesiastes 3:11 states, "God has set eternity in the human heart," meaning that we long for something more than what is offered on earth. When defining our purpose, we must extend our time horizon beyond our life on earth to our life after death. Limiting our purpose to the time we spend on earth is myopic. We should link our purpose to where we go after we die.

So where do you go after you die? Some people think you just cease to exist. They may ask, "If you didn't have any problem ceasing to exist before you were born, why should you have a problem ceasing to exist after you die?" Why don't we ponder life before birth? Why only life *after* death? Why is that terrifying to some?

Did you know that before you were born, you existed in the mind of God? To the prophet Jeremiah, God declared, "Before I formed you in the womb, I knew you, before you were born I set you apart; I appointed you as a prophet to the nations" (Jeremiah 1:5). So God had it all planned for Jeremiah before he was born. God does so for us as well. If we trace our existence before birth, we find God. If we trace our existence after death, we should likewise find God.

Some people claim we merely cease to exist when we die, but what is the proof for that? It is true that we disappear from this earth, but maybe we go to some other realm. Is there evidence that we go to another realm when we die? Yes. Good evidence.

There is one other consideration. If you plan to no longer exist when you die, what happens if you are wrong?

11

No, it is a much better strategy to plan on life after death. If you're right, you are prepared. If you're wrong and cease to exist at death, well, it won't really matter, will it?

Most people throughout human history have believed in life after death and the supernatural. A 2015 Pew Research poll found that 72 percent of Americans believe in heaven, and 58 percent believe in hell.[1] A 2019 YouGov poll revealed that 45 percent of Americans believe in ghosts and demons.[2] A 2016 Barna poll found that 66 percent of Americans believe in miracles and that God can heal people supernaturally.[3] In a two-volume book, *Miracles: The Credibility of the New Testament Accounts* (2011), Craig S. Keener wrote approximately a thousand pages carefully cataloging hundreds of miracles that occurred throughout the world, observed by very credible sources. It seems that miracles are much more common than we think. In the West, with our blind faith in the sciences, many people choose to ignore the supernatural.

Miracles are supernatural occurrences we cannot explain with the laws of nature that exist in our physical world. If there is a spiritual world, there must be a different set of laws with which we are unfamiliar. We can't explain occurrences in that realm … for now.

All throughout history, people have instinctively felt there is a spiritual realm. Is it mere superstition? You can fool some of the people some of the time, but can billions of people over time be wrong about their instincts? Are they all wrong that a realm beyond our own and a life after death exist? They may be wrong about *how* to get there but not that it exists.

Why not believe what the Bible says about life after death? It provides verifiable evidence to confirm whether or not it is true. There are hundreds of breadcrumbs to follow to verify the Bible's truthfulness. One other thing. The Bible provides the best explanation for what we observe in real life.

Here is a sampling of what the Bible says about heaven and hell in both the Old and New Testaments (emphasis added).

Heaven is God's holy dwelling place:

- "The priests and the Levites stood to bless the people, and God heard them, for their prayer reached *heaven*, his holy dwelling place" (2 Chronicles 30:27).

- "Then I said: 'Lord, the God of *heaven*, the great and awesome God, who keeps his covenant of love with those who love him and keep his commandments'" (Nehemiah 1:5).

- "Then God's temple in *heaven* was opened, and within his temple was seen the ark of his covenant. And there came flashes of lightning, rumblings, peals of thunder, an earthquake and a severe hailstorm" (Revelation 11:19).

Hell is a place of torment separated from God:

- "Multitudes who sleep in the dust of the earth will awake: some to everlasting life, others to *shame and everlasting contempt*" (Daniel 12:2).

- "The Son of Man will send out his angels, and they will weed out of his kingdom everything that causes sin and all who do evil. They will throw them into the *blazing furnace*, where there will be weeping and gnashing of teeth" (Matthew 13:41–42).

- "But the cowardly, the unbelieving, the vile, the murderers, the sexually immoral, those who practice magic arts, the idolaters and all liars—they will be consigned to the *fiery lake of burning sulfur*. This is the second death" (Revelation 21:8).

Many people today believe that all paths lead to heaven; you just have to be sincere about your beliefs. For example, if Muslims are sincere about their beliefs, then Muslims will go to heaven. If you sincerely believe that all good people will go to heaven and you are good, then you will go to heaven.

However, the latter belief seems to be an adult version of the contention that good little boys and girls will get presents from Santa Claus. For such an important question of where you go after death, we must agree that it takes more serious contemplation than that. Do people who think this way bother to consider what they are staking their eternal life on?

Lots of people are sincere about awful beliefs. Adolph Hitler was sincere about his beliefs. He acted out his beliefs in a logical manner. In Hitler's mind, he was genetically cleansing the earth to provide a better life for future generations. In his mind, it was similar to genetically breeding a superior strain of horses. To Hitler, his goals were noble. However, he was responsible for starting a war that killed about eighty-five million people, including six million Jews. Should he automatically go to heaven?

Hitler automatically going to heaven doesn't sound fair, so some beliefs sincerely held must not work as admittance requirements for heaven. Where is the cutoff? Which beliefs are valid and which are not? We think you'll agree that it is important to determine which beliefs are true and examine the evidence.

Evidence the Bible Is True

The Bible explicitly teaches that God created the heavens and the earth. God created space, time, matter, and energy—what science blithely attempts to explain away by calling it the *big bang*. Other religions, like Buddhism and Hinduism, have no definitive answer for the origin of the universe. The Buddha refused to provide an explanation, and Hindus have numerous theories that sometimes contradict one another. Only the Bible gives a clear-cut explanation for the origin of the universe. It was God, a being outside of time, space, and matter, who created it.

In addition, the Bible aligns accurately with reality. In particular, the Bible accurately depicts the moral condition of human beings. The Bible depicts humans as inherently and chronically sinful and not capable of perfecting themselves. In contrast, Buddhism and Hinduism teach that humans go through endless cycles of reincarnation until nirvana is reached. This is not what the Bible teaches. The Bible teaches that humans die once and then are judged. The only way to reach heaven is through Jesus Christ.

The Bible's account of humans' inherent and irredeemable sinfulness therefore predicts that all utopian schemes on earth, such as communism, will fail. Can that be verified? Yes. All utopian schemes have failed throughout history. The best evidence that humans are inherently sinful is the fact that parents do not have to teach their children to misbehave. Children do it naturally.

The Bible tells the story of the universe with a beginning, middle, and end. The story features the Jewish people as the unifying device. God bases the story of the universe around the Jewish people, who are called God's chosen people. God gave them the land of Israel. From the Jewish people came the Messiah Jesus, who died for the sins of humankind, rose from the dead, and ascended to heaven.

There will be a great tribulation someday, when the country of Israel will be attacked and saved only through God's intervention. At that time, Jesus will return and rule on earth for one thousand years from Jerusalem. After that, the entire heavens and earth will roll up in a fiery conflagration, and God will create a new heaven and earth, on which the saved will live forever, and the lost will be cast forever into the Lake of Fire.

God's Chosen People

The Jewish people are an important element throughout the Bible. Jesus was a Jew. The disciples were Jews, and the early church was filled with converted Jews. Since they are so important, shouldn't we find evidence today that the Jews are God's chosen people? Yes, indeed. Very dramatic evidence.

The Jewish religion is considered a major religion today, but do you know how many Jews there are in the entire world? Are there 2.1 billion, like the number of Christians? How about 1.3 billion Muslims or 900 million Hindus, or 376 million Buddhists? No. There are only fourteen million Jews in total in the entire world. Fourteen million!

Don't you think it is unusual for such a small number of people to receive such a big share of attention and hatred in the form of persecution and anti-Semitism? In the Middle Ages, Jews were expelled from European countries where they had settled after the Romans had expelled them from Palestine. In the 1940s, the Jews were nearly annihilated by the Nazis. It all makes sense, when you think of the Jews as God's chosen people. Satan and his evil forces, who are opposed to God, would certainly oppose God's chosen people.

Individual Jews are among the most successful and accomplished in history. They represent about 0.2 percent of the world's population yet comprise 23 percent of the Nobel Prize winners. Albert Einstein was a Jew. Half of the department stores in the US were started by or run by Jews, as were all the major Hollywood studios. Today, technology is the preeminent industry, with many companies founded by Jews, including Sergey Brin, cofounder of Google, Michael Dell, founder of Dell Computer, Andrew Grove, cofounder of Intel, and the list goes on and on.

Prophecies about the Jewish People

The Bible contains amazing prophecies about the Jewish people that have come true.

Promised Land. God promised the land of Israel and additional territory outside of Israel to Abraham in Genesis 15:18–21:

> On that day the Lord made a covenant with Abram and said, "To your descendants I give this land, from the Wadi of Egypt to the great river, the Euphrates— the land of the Kenites, Kenizzites, Kadmonites, Hittites, Perizzites, Rephaites, Amorites, Canaanites, Girgashites and Jebusites."

God reiterated this promise to Abraham's son Isaac (Genesis 26:3) and to Isaac's son Jacob (Genesis 28:13), who later became Israel after God changed Jacob's name. The Jews were driven out of their land in AD 70. They were almost annihilated in World War II. Today, they are miraculously back in the land God promised them and are prospering.

Dispersion of Jewish People. The dispersion of the Jews was predicted around seven hundred years before it happened in Deuteronomy 28:62–64:

You who were as numerous as the stars in the sky will be left but few in number, because you did not obey the Lord your God. Just as it pleased the Lord to make you prosper and increase in number, so it will please him to ruin and destroy you. You will be uprooted from the land you are entering to possess. Then the Lord will scatter you among all nations, from one end of the earth to the other. There you will worship other gods—gods of wood and stone, which neither you nor your ancestors have known.

The Jewish people, along with the Han Chinese, are two of the oldest intact people groups on earth. However, the Han Chinese were not driven from their country only to return again with their culture and identity intact, like the Jews. The Jews were driven out of their country three times, only to return for good after World War II, forming the nation of Israel in 1948. The three times were 733 BC by the Assyrians, 597 BC by the Babylonians, and AD 70 by the Romans.

Jewish People Would Stay Intact. The Bible predicted in Jeremiah 31:36–37, over two thousand years before it occurred, that the Jews would persevere as an intact people group despite the dispersion throughout the world:

> "Only if these decrees vanish from my sight," declares the Lord, "will Israel ever cease being a nation before me." This is what the Lord says: "Only if the heavens above can be measured and the foundations of the earth below be searched out will I reject all the descendants of Israel because of all they have done," declares the Lord.

Jewish People Would Return to the Land. The Bible also predicted in Isaiah 11:11–12 that the Jews would return to the land of Israel over two thousand years before it happened:

> In that day the Lord will reach out his hand a second time to reclaim the surviving remnant of his people

> from Assyria, from Lower Egypt, from Upper Egypt, from Cush, from Elam, from Babylonia, from Hamath and from the islands of the Mediterranean. He will raise a banner for the nations and gather the exiles of Israel; he will assemble the scattered people of Judah from the four quarters of the earth.

The nation of Israel is a miracle in itself. The day after it declared statehood in 1948, it was attacked by six Arab/Muslim countries and miraculously survived, although dramatically outnumbered and outgunned. Israel achieved two additional miraculous victories against those huge combined forces in 1967 and 1973.

Prophesies about Jesus

There are more than three hundred prophecies in the Old Testament that relate to Jesus.[4] Here are just eight.

1) *Arrival of the Messiah.* One of the most amazing prophecies is the exact timing in Daniel 9:24–25 when the Messiah, the Anointed One, will enter Jerusalem. This was written in around 530 BC, more than five hundred years before the event occurred:

> Seventy "sevens" are decreed for your people and your holy city to finish transgression, to put an end to sin, to atone for wickedness, to bring in everlasting righteousness, to seal up vision and prophecy and to anoint the Most Holy Place. Know and understand this: From the time the word goes out to restore and rebuild Jerusalem until the Anointed One, the ruler, comes, there will be seven "sevens," and sixty-two "sevens." It will be rebuilt with streets and a trench, but in times of trouble.

The "sevens" referred to in this verse are years. Seventy "sevens" are 490 years (70 x 7). The Anointed One will come in 483 years (7 + 62 = 69; 69 x 7 = 483). The Persian king Artaxerxes Longinonus authorized Nehemiah to go and rebuild Jerusalem, which started the clock. And

483 years later was Palm Sunday, when Jesus entered Jerusalem as a king. Daniel predicted the event to the exact year. (There is still one *seven* not yet fulfilled from the seventy referred to at the beginning of the verse. That seven has yet to occur. It is called the tribulation.)

John 12:12–13 describes the fulfillment of Daniel's Anointed One prophecy:

> The next day the great crowd that had come for the festival heard that Jesus was on his way to Jerusalem. They took palm branches and went out to meet him, shouting, "Hosanna! Blessed is he who comes in the name of the Lord! Blessed is the king of Israel!"

2) *Messiah born in Bethlehem.* The prophet Micah prophesized seven hundred years before the event in Micah 5:2 that Messiah Jesus would be born in Bethlehem:

> "But you, Bethlehem Ephrathah, though you are small among the clans of Judah, out of you will come for me one who will be ruler over Israel, whose origins are from of old, from ancient times."

The fulfillment is recorded in Matthew 2:1–6:

> After Jesus was born in Bethlehem in Judea, during the time of King Herod, Magi from the east came to Jerusalem and asked, "Where is the one who has been born king of the Jews? We saw his star when it rose and have come to worship him." When King Herod heard this he was disturbed, and all Jerusalem with him. When he had called together all the people's chief priests and teachers of the law, he asked them where the Messiah was to be born. "In Bethlehem in Judea," they replied, "for this is what the prophet has written: 'But you, Bethlehem, in the land of Judah, are by no means least among the rulers of Judah; for out of you will come a ruler who will shepherd my people Israel.'"

3) *Messiah Jesus born of a Virgin*. The prophet Isaiah prophesied seven hundred years before the fact in Isaiah 7:14 that Messiah Jesus would be born of a virgin:

> "Therefore the Lord himself will give you a sign: The virgin will conceive and give birth to a son, and will call him Immanuel."

The event was fulfilled and recorded in Matthew 1:20–23:

> But after he had considered this, an angel of the Lord appeared to him in a dream and said, "Joseph son of David, do not be afraid to take Mary home as your wife, because what is conceived in her is from the Holy Spirit. She will give birth to a son, and you are to give him the name Jesus, because he will save his people from their sins." All this took place to fulfill what the Lord had said through the prophet: "The virgin will conceive and give birth to a son, and they will call him Immanuel" (which means "God with us").

4) *Messiah Jesus tried and condemned*. Isaiah also predicted that Messiah Jesus would be tried and condemned in Isaiah 53:8:

> By oppression and judgment he was taken away. Yet who of his generation protested? For he was cut off from the land of the living; for the transgression of my people he was punished.

This was fulfilled as recorded in Matthew 27:1–2:

> Early in the morning, all the chief priests and the elders of the people made their plans how to have Jesus executed. So they bound him, led him away and handed him over to Pilate the governor.

5) *Messiah Jesus rejected by his own people*. Isaiah predicted that Messiah Jesus would be rejected by his own people in Isaiah 53:3:

> He was despised and rejected by mankind, a man of suffering, and familiar with pain. Like one from whom people hide their faces he was despised, and we held him in low esteem.

This was fulfilled and recorded in John 1:10–11:

> He was in the world, and though the world was made through him, the world did not recognize him. He came to that which was his own, but his own did not receive him.

6) *Messiah Jesus would die by crucifixion*. King David, one thousand years before the event, predicted that Messiah Jesus would die by crucifixion in Psalm 22:14–16:

> I am poured out like water, and all my bones are out of joint. My heart has turned to wax; it has melted within me. My mouth is dried up like a potsherd, and my tongue sticks to the roof of my mouth; you lay me in the dust of death. Dogs surround me, a pack of villains encircles me; they pierce my hands and my feet.

This was fulfilled and recorded in Matthew 27:31:

> After they had mocked him, they took off the robe and put his own clothes on him. Then they led him away to crucify him.

7) *Messiah Jesus would die as a sin offering*. This was predicted in Isaiah 53:5–6, 12:

> But he was pierced for our transgressions, he was crushed for our iniquities; the punishment that brought

21

us peace was on him, and by his wounds we are healed. We all, like sheep, have gone astray, each of us has turned to our own way; and the Lord has laid on him the iniquity of us all.

Therefore I will give him a portion among the great, and he will divide the spoils with the strong, because he poured out his life unto death, and was numbered with the transgressors. For he bore the sin of many, and made intercession for the transgressors.

The fulfillment, which we refer to as the Gospel, is recorded in 1 Corinthians 15:3–4:

For what I received I passed on to you as of first importance: that Christ died for our sins according to the Scriptures, that he was buried, that he was raised on the third day according to the Scriptures.

8) *Messiah Jesus would rise from the dead.* David records this prophecy in Psalm 16:10:

Because you will not abandon me to the realm of the dead, nor will you let your faithful one see decay.

The fulfillment is recorded in Matthew 28:5–7:

The angel said to the women, "Do not be afraid, for I know that you are looking for Jesus, who was crucified. He is not here; he has risen, just as he said. Come and see the place where he lay. Then go quickly and tell his disciples: 'He has risen from the dead and is going ahead of you into Galilee. There you will see him.' Now I have told you."

There were many other prophecies fulfilled by Jesus. We have examined eight. The odds of one person fulfilling just eight prophecies such as these is 1 in 100,000,000,000,000,000.[5] Scholars have identified hundreds of other prophecies, so this is a very convincing argument for the validity of the Bible.

Historical Accuracy

The Bible, especially the New Testament, was the most frequently copied and widely circulated books of antiquity. By comparison, Homer's *Iliad* was frequently copied and widely circulated, and we have 643 copies that exist today. The earliest copies that now exist were transcribed around 400 BC. Homer wrote the original manuscript five hundred years earlier in 900 BC. We can say that the earliest copies of Homer's *Iliad* were dated to within five hundred years of the original. Of course, the original manuscript has disintegrated and was lost over time. Only the copies remain, but nobody doubts the accuracy of the *Iliad*.

Compared to those 643 copies of the *Iliad*, the New Testament has at least 24,970 manuscript copies. Not all of these are complete copies of the New Testament. Some are, but many are individual books or fragments of books. Of the 24,970 copies, 5,366 are dated to within 225 years of the original manuscript. There are approximately 114 fragments dated to within fifty years of the original, two hundred whole books dated to within one hundred years, 250 copies of most of the New Testament dated to within 150 years, and 325 complete New Testament copies dated to within 225 years of the original.[6]

Consider that the copies of the US Constitution we have today are 233 years removed from the original document written in 1787. If the original document were destroyed, do you think the copies we have today are accurate despite the 233-year time span from the original? Yes, of course.

All of those copies of the New Testament can be compared to one another to detect copying errors in spelling, word choice, phrases inserted after the fact, and so on. Through this process of comparison, we can be very sure that the New Testament we hold in our hands is virtually identical to the original manuscripts written by the apostles.

One more point. The original manuscripts were written by eyewitnesses very soon after the recorded events. These manuscripts would have been rejected by those living at the time if those written accounts were fictitious.

Lastly, there is the miraculous account of Saul of Tarsus, who became the apostle Paul, the most significant of all Christian missionaries in history and author of nearly half of the books of the New Testament. For Saul of Tarsus to become the apostle Paul required a significant miracle. It would have been roughly equivalent to Osama bin Laden receiving a vision and converting to Christianity. That is what happened to Saul on his way to round up Christians in Damascus for arrest and possible execution.

Saul was a zealous pharisaical Jew who considered Christianity, then known as the Way, to be a blasphemous, heretical cult that must be stamped out. That is, until he encountered Jesus while on the road to Damascus. Paul was blinded for three days, had his vision restored by a Christian named Ananias, was baptized, and soon began preaching that Jesus is the Son of God. The whole transition could have taken as little as a week. The account is described in Acts 9. Only God could have converted Christianity's biggest enemy into its biggest promoter. This is just one of the many proofs that the Christian Bible is true and accurate.

Who are you going to believe? Choose the one who died and rose again. Jesus is alive. All other religious leaders throughout history are dead.

3

Visualizing Your Goals: What Is It Like in Heaven?

W ouldn't you agree that your ultimate destination should be heaven? We really only have two choices: heaven or hell. We will tell you how you can absolutely be sure you are going to heaven in chapter 4. Our purpose in this chapter is to describe what heaven is like, so you can have an image of it in your mind. This is important for goal setting. Goals must be specific, the S in SMART goals. They should be well defined, clear, and unambiguous. Therefore, you should be able to visualize your goals, to make them concrete, so you can persevere when obstacles appear.

God originally created a heaven-like earth for humans to live in, but sin entered the world, the world was cursed, and death resulted.

> In the beginning God created the heavens and the earth. (Genesis 1:1)

In the Garden of Eden, God placed two special trees: the tree of life and the tree of the knowledge of good and evil.

> The Lord God made all kinds of trees grow out of the ground—trees that were pleasing to the eye and good for food. In the middle of the garden were the tree of life and the tree of the knowledge of good and evil. (Genesis 2:9)

He forbade Adam to eat from the tree of the knowledge of good and evil. Then, God created Eve. The serpent deceived Eve, who ate the fruit from the tree and gave some to Adam to eat, even though he knew it was forbidden. God then cursed His creation after this and introduced death into the world.

> To Adam he said, "Because you listened to your wife and ate fruit from the tree about which I commanded you, 'You must not eat from it,' cursed is the ground because of you; through painful toil you will eat food from it all the days of your life. It will produce thorns and thistles for you, and you will eat the plants of the field. By the sweat of your brow you will eat your food

until you return to the ground, since from it you were taken; for dust you are and to dust you will return." (Genesis 3:17–19)

However, the good news is that sometime in the future (possibly sooner than you think, as we will discuss in chapter 5), God will transform the universe back to what He originally intended. God revealed this future transformation through the prophet Isaiah:

"See, I will create new heavens and a new earth. The former things will not be remembered, nor will they come to mind." (Isaiah 65:17)

More than seven hundred years later, God revealed this again to the apostle John in a vision. The new heaven and new earth will be Eden restored. The tree of life will appear again, but the tree of the knowledge of good and evil will be missing.

Then the angel showed me the river of the water of life, as clear as crystal, flowing from the throne of God and of the Lamb down the middle of the great street of the city. On each side of the river stood the tree of life, bearing twelve crops of fruit, yielding its fruit every month. And the leaves of the tree are for the healing of the nations. No longer will there be any curse. The throne of God and of the Lamb will be in the city, and his servants will serve him. (Revelation 22:1–3)

New Heaven = New Earth

Revelation 21 describes a new heaven and a new earth. Since God will dwell with His people, it seems logical that heaven and earth will merge, because God's residence is called heaven.

Then I saw "a new heaven and a new earth," for the first heaven and the first earth had passed away, and there was no longer any sea. I saw the Holy City, the new Jerusalem, coming down out of heaven from God, prepared as a bride beautifully dressed for her husband. And I heard a loud voice from the throne saying, "Look! God's dwelling place is now among the people, and he will dwell with them. They will be his people, and God himself will be with them and be their God." (Revelation 21:1–3)

Several verses in the Old Testament suggest that the earth will not be recreated but will be refurbished and enhanced. The reasoning is that God designated parts of the earth as an eternal inheritance. For example, God gave the land of Canaan, which is on the earth, to the children of Israel as an everlasting possession:

"I will establish my covenant as an everlasting covenant between me and you and your descendants after you for the generations to come, to be your God and the God of your descendants after you. The whole land of Canaan, where you now reside as a foreigner, I will give as an everlasting possession to you and your descendants after you; and I will be their God." (Genesis 17:7–8)

Jesus will reign on David's throne and kingdom, which are on earth:

Of the greatness of his government and peace there will be no end. He will reign on David's throne and over his kingdom, establishing and upholding it with justice and righteousness from that time on and forever. The zeal of the Lord Almighty will accomplish this. (Isaiah 9:7)

Terrain in Heaven

From a few hints in the Bible, we can infer that the terrain in heaven is like the present earth, with an atmosphere, mountains, water, trees, people, houses, cities, buildings, and streets. For example, John mentions physical objects we find on earth, such as a mountain and city in Revelation 21:10 and stones in Revelation 21:19a:

> And he carried me away in the Spirit to a mountain great and high, and showed me the Holy City, Jerusalem, coming down out of heaven from God. (Revelation 21:10)

> The foundations of the city walls were decorated with every kind of precious stone. (Revelation 21:19a)

The new heaven and new earth will contain countries and cities. These verses reference both a country and a city:

> People who say such things show that they are looking for a country of their own. If they had been thinking of the country they had left, they would have had opportunity to return. Instead, they were longing for a better country—a heavenly one. Therefore God is not ashamed to be called their God, for he has prepared a city for them. (Hebrews 11:14–16)

We are provided details about a specific city, New Jerusalem, described in Revelation 21:11, 16–19a, 23:

> It shone with the glory of God, and its brilliance was like that of a very precious jewel, like a jasper, clear as crystal.

> The city was laid out like a square, as long as it was wide. He measured the city with the rod and found it to be 12,000 stadia in length, and as wide and high as it is long. The angel measured the wall using human measurement, and it was 144 cubits thick. The wall was made of jasper, and the city of pure gold, as pure as glass. The foundations of the city walls were decorated with every kind of precious stone.

> The city does not need the sun or the moon to shine
> on it, for the glory of God gives it light, and the Lamb
> is its lamp.

According to the modern equivalents of the measures in Revelation 21, the city is 1,400 miles, long, wide, and high. The height would be the equivalent of 600,000 stories, and if the city were placed on the United States, the city would stretch north and south from Canada to Mexico and east and west from the Appalachian Mountains to the California border. Billions of people could live there with multiple square-mile lots per person.

A cube would resemble the Most Holy Place in the Temple described in 1 Kings 6:20. The inner sanctuary was twenty cubits long, twenty wide, and twenty high. Three dimensions is also suggestive of the three persons of the Trinity.

There are three gates on each side of the city, and each side is 1,400 miles long. Each gate may go out into a different country, perhaps each with different terrain. Everyone will have access to the city. People of different nationalities will go in and out of the city. Perhaps the gates will be places to gather and talk.

As Randy Alcorn speculates in his book *Heaven*, the new earth could be enhanced with features more spectacular than we have today. For example, on Mars, there is a volcano that is 79,000 feet tall, three times taller than Mount Everest. There is a valley on Mars that is 2,800 miles long, 370 miles wide, and 4.5 miles deep. Hundreds of our Grand Canyons could fit inside.[7] Perhaps God will incorporate features like these in the new earth.

The wall of the city is made of jasper, clear as crystal, and rests on a foundation with twelve layers, each decorated with precious stones. The city is constructed of pure gold, and the streets are also made of gold that is transparent as glass. The city will glow with perpetual light as it reflects the glory of God, which shines out through the clear jasper walls. The city may project a warm, golden glow as if from the sun. Picture the golden light streaming from the windows of a house as you approach at dusk and the warm and inviting sensation that provides.

Gold will be so plentiful it will be used as building material. The overall ambiance of the city will be enhanced by the visible foundation supporting the walls consisting of twelve layers decorated with precious stones, sparkling and glowing brilliantly with the following colors: blue (sapphire), sky blue (chalcedony), brilliant bright green (emerald), red and white (sardonyx), red and honey (sardius), transparent gold (chrysolite), sea green (beryl), yellow/green (topaz), green (chrysoprase), violet (jacinth), and purple (amethyst).

What Will It Be Like in Heaven?

In heaven, there is no crying because there is no grief, pain, suffering, or regret.

> He will wipe every tear from their eyes. There will be
> no more death or mourning or crying or pain, for the
> old order of things has passed away. (Revelation 21:4)

Jim Garlow, former pastor of Skyline Church and author of the book *Heaven and the Afterlife*, describes what he believes heaven will be like:

> If you want to know what heaven *feels* like, think of your
> deepest longings, those insatiable soul-cravings for love,
> acceptance, purpose, worth, intimacy, belonging. Now
> imagine what it would feel like to have those longings
> satisfied in a more abundant fashion than you've
> ever dreamed. Now multiply that feeling by infinity.
> Suddenly, heaven starts to sound exciting and enticing.[8]

Although not clearly stated in the Bible, Garlow says in heaven there might be plants, animals, music, games, major cities, buildings, art, culture, goods, services, major events, transportation, communication, education, learning, discovering, and leadership.[8]

We Will Have Resurrection Bodies Like Jesus

Jesus is described in the Bible as the First Fruits, a model of things to come. Jesus rose from the dead on the day we call Sunday. Back then, it was the sixteenth day of Nisan, the third day of Passover, and the first day of the Feast of First Fruits. The Passover lambs were sacrificed on the fourteenth day of Nisan, which was the day Jesus was crucified. He was the final sacrifice, the fulfillment of Passover, and called the Lamb of God.

First fruits refers to the first portion of the harvest that was given to God as specified in Deuteronomy 26:1–11. First fruits represents the first to come in chronological order, the hope of a greater harvest to follow, or something special dedicated to God. By giving God the first fruits, Israel acknowledged that all good things come from God.[9]

Jesus is our first fruits.

> But Christ has indeed been raised from the dead, the first fruits of those who have fallen asleep. For since death came through a man, the resurrection of the dead comes also through a man. For as in Adam all die, so in Christ all will be made alive. But each in turn: Christ, the first fruits; then, when he comes, those who belong to him. (1 Corinthians 15:20–23)

He therefore provides the model of our resurrected bodies in heaven.

> Dear friends, now we are children of God, and what we will be has not yet been made known. But we know that when Christ appears, we shall be like him, for we shall see him as he is. (1 John 3:2)

Our resurrected bodies will be like Jesus's body:

> Who, by the power that enables him to bring everything under his control, will transform our lowly bodies so that they will be like his glorious body. (Philippians 3:21)

Our resurrected bodies will be something fantastic:

> There are also heavenly bodies and there are earthly bodies; but the splendor of the heavenly bodies is one

kind, and the splendor of the earthly bodies is another. The sun has one kind of splendor, the moon another and the stars another; and star differs from star in splendor. So will it be with the resurrection of the dead. The body that is sown is perishable, it is raised imperishable; it is sown in dishonor, it is raised in glory; it is sown in weakness, it is raised in power; it is sown a natural body, it is raised a spiritual body. If there is a natural body, there is also a spiritual body. (1 Corinthians 15:40–44)

For those disabled or diseased on earth, they will be fully functional and healthy in heaven. Take Joni Eareckson Tada, a quadriplegic for fifty-three years, who suffered a devastating injury at the age of eighteen after diving into a shallow pool of water in Chesapeake Bay. An active child from an athletic family—her father was an Olympic wrestler—Joni has been confined to a wheelchair for all of these years.

She is a well-known evangelical Christian and founder of a ministry to the disabled called Joni and Friends. Joni looks forward to heaven. Maybe she will be a long-distance runner or swimmer there. Maybe a triathlete! She may host workout sessions.

The many years of disability will be in the past, shed like a butterfly exiting its cocoon. Imagine how she will enjoy her new body, feeling the muscles contracting and relaxing and responding to her every direction! She just may exercise for days at a time, savoring every minute.

Resurrected bodies can disappear and appear at will. Jesus was able to appear and disappear at will. The account is given in Luke 24. Several of Jesus's followers (one named Cleopas), on the Sunday Jesus rose from the dead, were walking on a road to a village called Emmaus, about seven miles from Jerusalem. As the followers were walking, they were suddenly joined by Jesus, but the Bible says, "They were kept from recognizing him." They may have seen Jesus crucified and die, or certainly had heard about it, so they were not expecting to see Jesus again.

Once they all reached Emmaus, they invited Jesus to stay the night. They probably went to one of their houses and sat down with Jesus to eat. We take up the account in Luke:

> When he was at the table with them, he took bread, gave thanks, broke it and began to give it to them. Then their eyes were opened and they recognized him, and he disappeared from their sight. They asked each other, "Were not our hearts burning within us while he talked with us on the road and opened the Scriptures to us?" (Luke 24:30–32)

Jesus simply vanished right before their eyes. These followers were so startled by seeing Jesus in the flesh and watching him disappear they immediately got up and walked the seven miles back to Jerusalem to tell the disciples. In a room where the eleven disciples were gathered, this happened next:

> While they were still talking about this, Jesus himself stood among them and said to them, "Peace be with you." They were startled and frightened, thinking they saw a ghost. (Luke 24:36–37)

We can receive some insight about our future resurrected bodies by the continued description of the event. Jesus's body was physical but different.

> He [Jesus] said to them, "Why are you troubled, and why do doubts rise in your minds? Look at my hands and my feet. It is I myself! Touch me and see; a ghost does not have flesh and bones, as you see I have." When he had said this, he showed them his hands and feet. (Luke 24:38–40)

Jesus's body could ingest food.

> And while they still did not believe it because of joy and amazement, he asked them, "Do you have anything here to eat?" They gave him a piece of broiled fish, and he took it and ate it in their presence. (Luke 24:41–43)

Food in Heaven

We will eat in heaven. Just as Jesus was able to eat in his resurrection body, so will we be able to eat in our resurrected bodies. On another occasion after Jesus's resurrection, he ate with his disciples, this time not long before he ascended to heaven:

> Jesus said to them, "Bring some of the fish you have just caught." So Simon Peter climbed back into the boat and dragged the net ashore. It was full of large fish, 153, but even with so many the net was not torn. Jesus said to them, "Come and have breakfast." None of the disciples dared ask him, "Who are you?" They knew it was the Lord. Jesus came, took the bread and gave it to them, and did the same with the fish. This was now the third time Jesus appeared to his disciples after he was raised from the dead. (John 21:10–14)

We have previously read that in heaven, the tree of life will bear twelve crops of fruit to eat. In addition, there is a vast supper mentioned in the Bible that will take place in heaven for all of the believers there. So it definitely indicates we will enjoy food in heaven:

> Then the angel said to me, "Write this: Blessed are those who are invited to the wedding supper of the Lamb!" And he added, "These are the true words of God." (Revelation 19:9)

Work in Heaven

We can work in heaven. God designed us to work and provided work before the Fall; only then, the work was not frustrating and tedious. It was only after the Fall that it became so.

> The Lord God took the man and put him in the Garden of Eden to work it and take care of it. (Genesis 2:15)

In heaven, there will also be work and responsibilities. It says that believers will reign with Christ, our King, and have authority over nations of people. We will also serve God and Jesus.

> If we endure, we will also reign with him. If we disown him, he will also disown us. (2 Timothy 2:12)

> To the one who is victorious and does my will to the end, I will give authority over the nations. (Revelation 2:26)

> No longer will there be any curse. The throne of God and of the Lamb will be in the city, and his servants will serve him. (Revelation 22:3)

Rest in Heaven

There will be rest from our work. Work will be meaningful and interesting, but we will not work all the time. We will enjoy rest from work, perfect and pleasing relaxation:

> Then I heard a voice from heaven say, "Write this: Blessed are the dead who die in the Lord from now on." "Yes," says the Spirit, "they will rest from their labor, for their deeds will follow them." (Revelation 14:13b)

The new country will be a real utopia, something humans have aspired to create over thousands of years. All utopian attempts on earth have failed, but utopia in heaven will be the real thing. The reason? The new heaven and new earth is filled with the knowledge of God:

> For the earth will be filled with the knowledge of the glory of the LORD as the waters cover the sea. (Habakkuk 2:14)

4

Are You Going To Heaven?

Heaven is a fantastic place, for sure, a destination to *die for*. A recipe on the internet claimed that their pot roast was something to die for. If we can eagerly look forward to pot roast for dinner, how much more so should we look forward to heaven? Now, the question is, Who gets to go?

Some say everybody gets to go. That's universalism, but is it true? Does Adolf Hitler automatically get to go? That hardly seems fair to the eighty-five million people who died in World War II, a war Hitler started. How about the more than six million Jews killed in the death camps? Would they think Hitler deserved to go to heaven?

Since heaven is where God lives, shouldn't we first learn as much as we can about Him? After all, we will spend eternity with Him. People get married to live together for a lifetime. They certainly take the time to find out what their partners are like! How much more so should we find out what God is like? We will live with Him for eternity, not just a lifetime.

The well-known theologian R.C. Sproul, in his book *The Holiness of God*, points out the following:

> Only once in sacred Scripture is an attribute of God elevated to the third degree. Only once is a characteristic of God mentioned three times in succession. The Bible says God is holy, holy, holy. Not that He is merely holy, or even holy, holy. He is holy, holy, holy. The Bible never says that God is love, love, love; or mercy, mercy, mercy; or wrath, wrath, wrath; or justice, justice, justice. It does say that He is holy, holy, holy, that the whole earth is full of His glory.[10]

The verses Sproul is referring to are these:

> Above him were seraphim, each with six wings: With two wings they covered their faces, with two they covered their feet, and with two they were flying. And they were calling to one another: "Holy, holy, holy is the

> LORD Almighty; the whole earth is full of his glory."
> (Isaiah 6:2–3)

> Each of the four living creatures had six wings and was
> covered with eyes all around, even under its wings. Day
> and night they never stop saying: "'Holy, holy, holy is
> the Lord God Almighty,' who was, and is, and is to
> come." (Revelation 4:8)

Is it any wonder that the Hymn Society in the United States and
Canada named the hymn "Holy, Holy, Holy" by Reginald Heber and
John Bacchus Dykes as the greatest hymn of all time?[11]

It is interesting to note the reactions of people in the Bible when
they came into the presence of God. Let's notice how three of the most
prominent prophets in the Bible, Isaiah, Ezekiel, and the apostle John,
reacted when they encountered God through powerful visions when
heaven was opened up and revealed to them:

> "Woe to me!" I cried. "I am ruined! For I am a man of
> unclean lips, and I live among a people of unclean lips,
> and my eyes have seen the King, the LORD Almighty."
> (Isaiah 6:5)

> Like the appearance of a rainbow in the clouds on a
> rainy day, so was the radiance around him. This was
> the appearance of the likeness of the glory of the LORD.
> When I saw it, I fell facedown, and I heard the voice of
> one speaking. (Ezekiel 1:28)

> When I saw him, I fell at his feet as though dead. Then
> he placed his right hand on me and said: "Do not be
> afraid. I am the First and the Last." (Revelation 1:17)

The holiness of God produces fear and awe. So what is holiness?
Sproul explains that holy conveys "separate" but is also transcendent,
something "far above and beyond us." It also conveys purity.

When God designates something as holy, it is separate and special.

He is very particular about holy things. He instructed Moses to take his sandals off in front of the burning bush:

> "Do not come any closer," God said. "Take off your sandals, for the place where you are standing is holy ground." (Exodus 3:5)

God was very detailed when He instructed the Israelites, after they were freed from Pharaoh, to build the tabernacle (tent) in Exodus 25–27 and the Ark of the Covenant (sacred carrying box to hold the Ten Commandments and other sacred objects) in Exodus 37. They were to build the objects exactly as God instructed. To carry the ark, two poles were inserted into rings on either side so no human would touch the ark (Exodus 25:12–14; Numbers 4:15). When a man named Uzzah touched the ark to keep it from tipping over when improperly transported on a cart, God struck him dead (2 Samuel 6:1–7).

God takes holiness seriously. He is 100 percent pure, 100 percent holy. How do you think He would think about future residents of heaven who don't care about His holiness or His rules?

Let's say you have a mansion on a Caribbean island that was your dream house. You are thinking of inviting some friends to live with you for the winter. Would you want people who tracked mud into their own house, threw their dirty clothes on their floors, and jumped up and down on their couch? You would be careful who you invited. A winter is only a couple of months. Think about eternity.

Before you begin to think that God is like that cranky aunt who says that you cannot play in the living room, consider this. Who invented play? God. Do you need to teach a child how to play? Who invented laughter? God. Do you need to teach a baby how to laugh? Who invented dreaming and creativity? God. Do you need to teach children how to imagine?

God is holy and takes sin seriously. Shouldn't we? The apostle Peter instructs us:

> But just as he who called you is holy, so be holy in all
> you do; for it is written: "Be holy, because I am holy."
> (1 Peter 1:15–16)

Here on earth, we cannot be as holy as God, but we certainly can submit to Him and obey. The things designated by God to be holy should be used in a proper way. A husband and wife have been designated by God to have sex. They have been set apart in holy marriage. Therefore, it is sinful to have sex in any other context, such as premarital or same-sex relationships.

Does God Grade on a Curve?

Many people, like Muslims, believe God grades on a scale, weighing your good and bad deeds. If the good deeds outweigh the bad, you go to heaven. Otherwise, you go to hell.

Let's say you need to reach thirty thousand good deeds in your lifetime, about one per day for eighty years. You die and come before God, and you only have 29,999. You plead with God that it isn't fair that only one missing deed should keep you from spending eternity in heaven. He agrees and sets the bar at 29,999. Then, another person with 29,998 pleads with God with the same reasoning. God lowers it to 29,997; someone pleads, then God lowers it to 29,996; and so on, until the cut-off point is zero. God says this won't do. He can't automatically admit everybody, including Hitler.

Therefore, He goes the other way; He increases the cutoff point to 30,001. The person who has 30,000 pleads, so God raises it to 30,002, then 30,003, and so on. This goes on until the goal is so high nobody gets in using good deeds as the entrance requirement. This is the standard God finally selects. Nobody enters heaven based on their good deeds.

Can you see that it doesn't make sense to use good deeds as the criteria for admission to an eternal heaven? Ultimately some people will be short one good deed. Would it be fair to keep a person from going to heaven, which is forever, because that person was missing one good deed?

The logic of this argument applies to saying, "I'm basically a good person" or "all good people go to heaven." What are the precise criteria to use? What is the cutoff point? You can see the problem of basing time spent in eternity (numberless) on a finite number of works.

Something else to consider is sin. Sin is like bacteria, which multiplies and grows. Heaven contains no sin (bacteria). Therefore, it is a 100 percent sterile environment. No sin can enter. None. This is important because heaven is eternal. One bacterium over time—say ten thousand years—could contaminate the whole place. God is very particular about His environment and who He lives with for such a long period of time. God requires a sin-free environment. Who then can enter sin-free? We are, after all, sinful people.

Nevertheless, God wants people to live with Him. The apostle Peter states:

> The Lord is not slow in keeping his promise, as some understand slowness. Instead he is patient with you, not wanting anyone to perish, but everyone to come to repentance. (2 Peter 3:9)

God doesn't want anyone to perish (not go to heaven), but He and heaven are sin-free, so what can He do? He will provide the only good deed that will count, something done by Himself. He, an eternal being, will personally give His life as a sacrifice for the sins of humans by coming to earth in the form of a man, Jesus. An eternal being can provide the suitable payment for entry into an eternal kingdom.

So, does that mean that everybody now gets in? Does Jesus's death cover everybody automatically? No. A gift given must be received. Let's say your friend leaves at the will-call window a ticket he bought for you to attend a football game or concert. Can you just walk into the stadium? No. You must first pick up the ticket at the will-call window. Once you have received it, you may enter the stadium.

How to Be Saved

So how does a person receive the payment that God gave through Jesus? How can a person be saved? Think of it as a four-step process that the great evangelist Billy Graham offered to the thousands of people attending his more than four hundred crusades that he conducted over his lifetime to more than 215 million people around the world. Here is Billy, and his son Franklin, Graham's, four-step process:[12]

1. Admit you are a sinner and need a savior.

We are all sinners (infected with "bacteria") and cannot enter God's sin-free environment:

> For all have sinned and fall short of the glory of God. (Romans 3:23)

There is a gulf between us and God that we cannot bridge on our own. Left to ourselves, we face judgment and eternal separation from God, as displayed in figure 1.

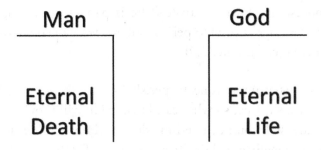

Figure 1. Man is separated from God.

2. Repent, which is changing your attitude and the direction of your life by turning away from your sins, as Jesus instructs:

> Jesus answered them, "It is not the healthy who need a doctor, but the sick. I have not come to call the righteous, but sinners to repentance." (Luke 5:31–32)

The apostle Peter, speaking to a crowd after Jesus's resurrection, said this:

Repent, then, and turn to God, so that your sins may be wiped out, that times of refreshing may come from the Lord. (Acts 3:19)

3. Believe that Jesus died for your sins and was raised from the dead:

For God so loved the world that he gave his one and only Son, that whoever believes in him shall not perish but have eternal life. (John 3:16)

Jesus is the only way to heaven. There is no other way. Just being sincere or having good intentions won't work. Just being a good person won't work. Just being a Buddhist, Hindu, Muslim, or Jew won't work. Only Jesus's death on the cross will work. This is displayed in Figure 2.

Jesus answered, "I am the way and the truth and the life. No one comes to the Father except through me." (John 14:6)

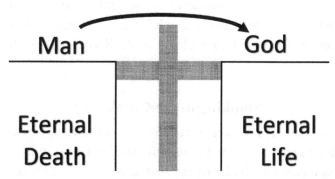

Figure 2. Man is reconciled to God.

There is nothing we can do on our own. All we can do is accept the payment Jesus made on our behalf. He paid the ticket for admission to heaven.

> For it is by grace you have been saved, through faith—
> and this is not from yourselves, it is the gift of God—not
> by works, so that no one can boast. (Ephesians 2:8–9)

4. Receive Jesus as your Lord and Savior. You can do this by
    praying as suggested below, when you will invite Jesus to enter
    into and control your life through the Holy Spirit. Here is a
    sample prayer provided by Billy and Franklin Graham:

    > Dear Lord Jesus, I know that I am a sinner and need
    > Your forgiveness. I believe that You died for my sins. I
    > want to turn from my sins. I now invite You to come
    > into my heart and life. I want to trust and follow You as
    > Lord and Savior. In Jesus' name. Amen.[12]

So how can a person be saved?

> If you declare with your mouth, "Jesus is Lord," and
> believe in your heart that God raised him from the
> dead, you will be saved. For it is with your heart that you
> believe and are justified, and it is with your mouth that
> you profess your faith and are saved. (Romans 10:9–10)

Smoking or Nonsmoking

Years ago, before smoking restrictions, there were smoking and
nonsmoking areas designated in restaurants, airplanes, and so on. The
same choice exists in the hereafter: hell or heaven. The choice is ours.
Either we choose nonsmoking, eternal life in heaven with a holy God
who paid the price for our admission through the death of His Son,
Jesus, or we choose smoking, eternal torment in hell.

Many people object to this notion, that God would send anyone to
hell. However, God is not doing the choosing; people are making the
choice. They either accept Jesus as Savior, or they don't.

Remember, God created us in *His* image. Many people today have
created God in *their* image. They have created a God that ignores sin

and admits "good" people into heaven. However, the definition of *good* is unknown, so it is anyone's guess if he or she can enter heaven. Sort of like rolling the dice. They also believe God ignores sin. It makes Him more like us, sort of fickle. Taken to the extreme, God becomes more like the gods of the ancient Romans.

Roman gods didn't care about the morality of the people. Roman gods were vengeful and even deceitful. Their moods could swing unexpectedly. Therefore, the Romans were careful to humor their gods and appease their tempers by paying tribute through specific rituals. It was essentially paying bribes to the gods to get them to do what the people wanted.

The true God is not like that. He is not erratic. His rules are clearly stated. He does not take bribes. His character is wholly consistent. He is 100 percent holy and 100 percent just, with a justice that is wholly consistent with His holy character.

God's standard is perfection. Only a payment from an infinite being can buy admission to an infinite environment. Only the death of an infinite being is a worthy sacrifice for sin.

Ultimately, people who make up their own rules, who create God in their own image and are proud and wink at their own and others' sins, have no need for God. They will not be happy in heaven. Therefore, God allows them to make the decision to live forever apart from Him.

What Happens When You Are Saved?

So, what happens when you are saved? When we accept Jesus Christ as our Savior, our sins are forgiven; we have assurance we will go to heaven; we are viewed by God as saints, not sinners; we are adopted into God's family; and we are indwelt by the Holy Spirit.

Sins forgiven. Once you accept Jesus as Lord and Savior, your sins are forgiven:

> In him we have redemption through his blood, the forgiveness of sins, in accordance with the riches of God's grace. (Ephesians 1:7)

Assurance of heaven. Once you accept Jesus as Lord and Savior, you can be certain you will go to heaven:

> Whoever believes in the Son has eternal life, but whoever rejects the Son will not see life, for God's wrath remains on them. (John 3:36)

> I give them eternal life, and they shall never perish; no one will snatch them out of my hand. (John 10:28)

Viewed as saints. Once you accept Jesus as Lord and Savior, you are viewed by God as a saint (holy people), not a sinner. This is not by your efforts but is by Jesus's sacrifice:

> Paul and Timothy, servants of Christ Jesus, To all God's holy people in Christ Jesus at Philippi, together with the overseers and deacons. (Philippians 1:1)

Adopted into God's family. Once you accept Jesus as Lord and Savior, you are adopted into the family of God:

> Consequently, you are no longer foreigners and strangers, but fellow citizens with God's people and also members of his household. (Ephesians 2:19)

Indwelling Holy Spirit. Once you accept Jesus as Lord and Savior, you receive the indwelling Holy Spirit:

> You, however, are not in the realm of the flesh but are in the realm of the Spirit, if indeed the Spirit of God lives in you. And if anyone does not have the Spirit of Christ, they do not belong to Christ. But if Christ is in you, then even though your body is subject to death because of sin, the Spirit gives life because of righteousness. And if the Spirit of him who raised Jesus from the dead is living in you, he who raised Christ from the dead will

also give life to your mortal bodies because of his Spirit who lives in you. (Romans 8:9–11)

Trinity

The Holy Spirit is the third person of the Trinity (Father, Son, Holy Spirit). We believe in one God, who is three distinct persons, all of whom are God:

Father. This verse refers to the Father as God:

> Grace and peace to you from God our Father and the Lord Jesus Christ. (Philippians 1:2)

Son. This verse refers to Jesus as God:

> While we wait for the blessed hope—the appearing of the glory of our great God and Savior, Jesus Christ. (Titus 2:13)

Holy Spirit. This verse refers to the Holy Spirit as God:

> Then Peter said, "Ananias, how is it that Satan has so filled your heart that you have lied to the Holy Spirit and have kept for yourself some of the money you received for the land? Didn't it belong to you before it was sold? And after it was sold, wasn't the money at your disposal? What made you think of doing such a thing? You have not lied just to human beings but to God." (Acts 5:3–4)

The Holy Spirit is our counselor and lives inside of us. We still have freewill, but we do not want to grieve the Holy Spirit. He establishes His temple inside of us, teaches and prompts us, intercedes for us and helps us to pray, equips us to share the Gospel, conveys desirable characteristics to us, and guarantees our transmission to heaven.

Temple of the Holy Spirit. The temple is no longer an external physical structure but is resident inside of every believer. (We should, therefore, not practice sexual immorality.)

> Do you not know that your bodies are temples of the Holy Spirit, who is in you, whom you have received from God? You are not your own. (1 Corinthians 6:19)

Teacher and Prompter. The Holy Spirit will teach us how to live godly lives and bring the teaching of the Bible to mind when we need it:

> But the Advocate, the Holy Spirit, whom the Father will send in my name, will teach you all things and will remind you of everything I have said to you. (John 14:26)

Intercessor. The Holy Spirit helps us to pray and even intercedes (prays) for us:

> In the same way, the Spirit helps us in our weakness. We do not know what we ought to pray for, but the Spirit himself intercedes for us through wordless groans. (Romans 8:26)

Equipper. The Holy Spirit conveys power to spread the Gospel:

> But you will receive power when the Holy Spirit comes on you; and you will be my witnesses in Jerusalem, and in all Judea and Samaria, and to the ends of the earth. (Acts 1:8)

Conveyor. The Holy Spirit conveys desirable characteristics in our lives that set us apart:

> But the fruit of the Spirit is love, joy, peace, forbearance, kindness, goodness, faithfulness, gentleness and self-control. Against such things there is no law. (Galatians 5:22–23)

Guarantor. The Holy Spirit seals us, much like a preservative, and guarantees our transmission from this life to heaven:

> And you also were included in Christ when you heard the message of truth, the gospel of your salvation. When you believed, you were marked in him with a seal, the promised Holy Spirit, who is a deposit guaranteeing our inheritance until the redemption of those who are God's possession—to the praise of his glory. (Ephesians 1:13–14)

Humans consist of three components, somewhat analogous to the Trinity: body, soul, and spirit, as shown by Figure 3 on the next page. The body will die, but the soul and spirit live on. We are souls who have physical bodies. The spirit is an inner force that directs a person toward or away from God. In this physical world, our spirit is sinful and influenced by Satan, and by default, our soul and spirit will go to hell (left side of Figure 3). If we accept Jesus Christ as Savior, the Holy Spirit indwells us, and our soul and spirit will go to heaven (right side of Figure 3). Our sinful nature is left behind, like the dirt left behind on the floor of a car wash. Jesus is the one who cleanses us from sin.

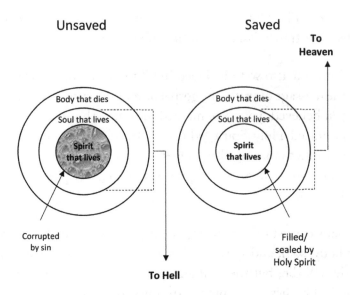

Figure 3. Body, soul, and spirit at death

The Purpose of Life

The goal of life is to go to heaven and to earn rewards during life on earth that are redeemed in heaven. What is the purpose of life? Earning rewards is the manifestation of that purpose, but what is the actual purpose?

The Westminster Shorter Catechism states it succinctly: "Man's chief end is to glorify God and to enjoy Him forever." So how do we glorify God with our lives? We glorify God through our holy conduct, conduct that is set apart or special.

We glorify God by having faith in His promises. An example is Abraham, who at the age of one hundred was told by God that Abraham would produce a son with his equally aged wife, Sarah, and through this bloodline would come the Messiah. Abraham believed that God could and would do it. Because Abraham believed, he gave glory to God:

> Yet he [Abraham] did not waver through unbelief regarding the promise of God, but was strengthened in his faith and gave glory to God. (Romans 4:20)

We glorify God through worship, by acknowledging His power, majesty, and love, and by expressing gratefulness to Him:

> Praise the LORD, all you nations; extol him, all you peoples. For great is his love toward us, and the faithfulness of the LORD endures forever. Praise the LORD. (Psalm 117:1–2)

We glorify God when we use the spiritual gifts He bestows on us to serve others:

> Each of you should use whatever gift you have received to serve others, as faithful stewards of God's grace in its various forms. If anyone speaks, they should do so as one who speaks the very words of God. If anyone serves, they should do so with the strength God provides, so that in all things God may be praised through Jesus Christ. To him be the glory and the power for ever and ever. Amen. (1 Peter 4:10–11)

Through holy living, we should seek to bring glory to God. By doing this, we develop an eternal perspective and set our minds on heavenly things, on our goals:

> Since, then, you have been raised with Christ, set your hearts on things above, where Christ is, seated at the right hand of God. Set your minds on things above, not on earthly things. (Colossians 3:1–2)

Paul provides specific rules for holy living in the remaining verses of Colossians 3. Do not engage in sexual immorality, impurity, lust, evil desires, and greed. Rid yourselves of anger, rage, malice, slander, and filthy language. Do not lie to one another. Be filled with compassion, kindness, humility, gentleness, and patience. Forgive one another. Be thankful to God.

We can keep our minds on heavenly things and acquire the right motivation to earn rewards in heaven when we follow the advice in verse 17:

> And whatever you do, whether in word or deed, do it all in the name of the Lord Jesus, giving thanks to God the Father through him.

5

Timeline for Heaven

To employ SMART goals, you must assign completion dates to your subgoals and final goal. Of course, this is not possible when discussing heaven because we do not know when we will die. Only God knows when we will die. God knows us intimately, even to the extent of numbering the hairs on our head, as the following verse reveals:

> Are not two sparrows sold for a penny? Yet not one of them will fall to the ground outside your Father's care. And even the very hairs of your head are all numbered. So don't be afraid; you are worth more than many sparrows. (Matthew 10:29–31)

The verse states that a tiny sparrow dies (falls to the ground) only under God's direction. If He decided when a sparrow dies, would He not decide when we, as humans made in His image, die? In the book of Psalms, David writes that God knew us before we were born and has determined how many days we will live (all the days ordained for me), as revealed in the following verse:

> Your eyes saw my unformed body; all the days ordained for me were written in your book before one of them came to be. (Psalm 139:16)

However, the Bible prophetically reveals that a sequence of events in history must take place before we reach our final destination, what the Bible calls the new heaven and new earth. This sequence of events is displayed in Figure 4, a prophecy timeline, which we will explain in this chapter.

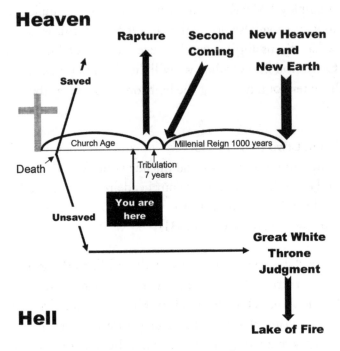

Figure 4. Prophecy timeline.

Saved versus Unsaved

When we die, we go to one of two places: heaven for those who are saved and hell for those who are unsaved. Frequently, Christians refer to someone who is born again as "saved." *Born again* and *saved* both refer to a person who has personally accepted Jesus as their Savior and Lord. Accepting Jesus as Savior means that you trust in Jesus's sacrifice on the cross alone for your salvation:

> Jesus answered, "I am the way and the truth and the life. No one comes to the Father except through me." (John 14:6)

You have admitted that you have no merit before God. There is nothing you can do on your own that will make you worthy to spend eternity with a holy God. Nothing. The high price of admission to heaven cannot be paid by you. Only Jesus's death can pay that price.

For it is by grace you have been saved, through faith—
and this is not from yourselves, it is the gift of God—not
by works, so that no one can boast. (Ephesians 2:8–9)

Jesus's death was the fulfillment of the sacrificial system God
initiated for the Israelites to atone for their sins. It required a blood
sacrifice. It is blood that gives life. The blood sacrifice atones for sin.

For the life of a creature is in the blood, and I have
given it to you to make atonement for yourselves on the
altar; it is the blood that makes atonement for one's life.
(Leviticus 17:11)

On the Day of Atonement, Yom Kippur, described in Leviticus
16, the Israelites were to perform an annual sacrifice for the sins of the
people. The high priest would select two goats. One goat would be
sacrificed and its blood sprinkled on the Ark of the Covenant (a special
chest containing sacred objects, such as the Ten Commandments). The
other goat would be the scapegoat. The high priest would confess the
sins of the people over the scapegoat and release it into the wilderness,
carrying on itself the sins of the people.

Offering a blood sacrifice was first required during the Exodus of
the Israelites from Egypt at the first Passover described in Exodus 12.
Each family was to choose a male lamb without defect. They were to
slaughter the lamb at twilight and take some of the blood and spread it
on the sides and top of the doorframes of their houses. Then, the angel
of death would pass over the house. The Israelites were to eat the lamb
and prepare to leave Egypt. This observance was repeated annually by
the Jewish people for about 1,500 years. It reminded them that God
saved them from slavery and that they passed from death to life.

This sacrifice foreshadowed Jesus's death on the cross, which allows
us to pass from death to eternal life.

For the wages of sin is death, but the gift of God is
eternal life in Christ Jesus our Lord. (Romans 6:23)

Without the shedding of blood, there is no forgiveness of sin.

> God presented Christ as a sacrifice of atonement, through the shedding of his blood—to be received by faith. He did this to demonstrate his righteousness, because in his forbearance he had left the sins committed beforehand unpunished. (Romans 3:25)

Blood gives life, and sin causes death. God sacrificed Himself through Jesus Christ and shed His own blood to pay for our sins—past, present, and future—and to grant us eternal life.

Jesus became the final sacrifice, the final sacrifice for all time. He, like the Passover lamb, was unblemished, without sin. That is why John the Baptist called Jesus the Lamb of God:

> The next day John saw Jesus coming toward him and said, "Look, the Lamb of God, who takes away the sin of the world!" (John 1:29)

Jesus was crucified on Passover; at the same time, the Passover lamb was sacrificed in the temple. Thirty-seven years after the crucifixion, the temple, where the sacrifices took place for Passover and Yom Kippur, was destroyed by the Romans in AD 70. Coincidence? The Jews were no longer able to make sacrifices for sins. As Christians, we know that it was no longer necessary because Jesus became the final sacrifice.

You can claim that payment by: 1) believe that Jesus died and rose from the dead and prepares a place for you in heaven; 2) admit you are a sinner unworthy of heaven and that only Jesus's death on the Cross can pay for your sins; 3) accept Jesus's payment on the cross; and 4) trust in Jesus's payment on the cross alone for admission to heaven. This is called the Gospel and is summarized in the following verses:

> Now, brothers and sisters, I want to remind you of the gospel I preached to you, which you received and on which you have taken your stand. By this gospel you are saved, if you hold firmly to the word I preached to you. Otherwise, you have believed in vain. For what I

received I passed on to you as of first importance: that Christ died for our sins according to the Scriptures, that he was buried, that he was raised on the third day according to the Scriptures. (1 Corinthians 15:1–4)

Those who believe in Jesus will have eternal life:

For God so loved the world that he gave his one and only Son, that whoever believes in him shall not perish but have eternal life. (John 3:16)

Heaven

When we die and we are saved, we immediately go into the presence of Jesus in heaven. However, as you can see to the far right in Figure 4, shown a few pages back, ultimately, we will live in a new heaven and new earth. That will be our final destination. However, before we arrive there, several events must take place.

For now, at death, we are instantly transported to heaven. Jesus on the cross assured one of the thieves that the thief would go to heaven instantly. It was the thief who asked Jesus to remember him when Jesus came into His kingdom. Here is how Jesus replied:

Jesus answered him, "Truly I tell you, today you will be with me in paradise." (Luke 23:43)

Paul in the following verses states that once we die, we come immediately into the presence of Jesus:

We are confident, I say, and would prefer to be away from the body and at home with the Lord. (2 Corinthians 5:8)

I am torn between the two: I desire to depart and be with Christ, which is better by far. (Philippians 1:23)

Hell

Those who are unsaved, who trust in anything other than Jesus Christ for their salvation, are cast into hell. All humans are inherently sinful and by default condemned by God. Those who do not believe in Jesus remain condemned:

> Whoever believes in him is not condemned, but whoever does not believe stands condemned already because they have not believed in the name of God's one and only Son. (John 3:18)

As fallen humans, sinners all, we are condemned to hell because God is a holy God. However, God has provided a means to avoid condemnation if we believe in Jesus, trust in His payment for our sins alone to save us, and turn from (repent of) our sins.

At death, those not believing in and trusting in Jesus are sent to hell and ultimately into the Lake of Fire, where unbelievers and Satan and his demons will be sent as a consequence of the Great White Throne Judgment at the end of the millennial reign of Jesus.

Before Jesus's payment for sins on the cross, hell, the destination of the dead, contained two places separated by an unbridgeable chasm. There was Abraham's Bosom and Hell. Abraham's Bosom was a place where Old Testament believers went when they died. They remained there until Christ died for their sins and led them out to heaven.

> This is why it says: "When he ascended on high, he took many captives and gave gifts to his people." (What does "he ascended" mean except that he also descended to the lower, earthly regions?) (Ephesians 4:8–9)

Hell is the setting for the following account, apparently not a parable, that Jesus describes in Luke 16:19–31. In life, a rich man ignored a beggar named Lazarus, who was covered with sores and laid at the rich man's gate, hoping to eat what fell from the rich man's table. Both died. Lazarus was taken to Abraham's Bosom, and the rich man was taken to hell (Hades). Luke describes it here:

In Hades, where he was in torment, he looked up and
saw Abraham far away, with Lazarus by his side. (Luke
16:23)

The rich man, thinking he was still in charge, asks Abraham to
have pity on him and to send Lazarus to dip his finger in water and
cool the rich man's tongue because the rich man was "in agony in this
fire." Abraham replied that no one can cross the chasm, and all the
comfort the rich man could expect was over, previously enjoyed when
he was alive.

Then the rich man begs Abraham to send Lazarus (the rich man
still thinks of Lazarus as some sort of personal servant) to warn his
brothers, who are still living. Abraham replies that the brothers have
the scriptures (Moses and the prophets) to read, which explain how to
avoid hell. If they will not believe the scriptures, they are so hardened
that they won't even believe someone who has risen from the dead, no
doubt rationalizing that the resurrected person never died to begin with.

Church Age

Bible history can be divided into two periods, much like the Bible is
divided into the Old and New Testaments. The two periods are the Age
of the Law, corresponding to the Old Testament, and the Church Age,
corresponding to the New Testament.

The Age of the Law was meant to show humans that, without faith
in God's promises (including a coming Messiah) and empowerment
of the Holy Spirt, they could not obey God and fully obey the laws
that God gave to Moses. They would surely fall short and require a
Savior. The Church Age is called the Age of Grace because of Jesus's
substitutionary death on the cross for our sins as the promised Savior.
By accepting His substitutionary payment for our sins, we are provided
the indwelling Holy Spirit, who will guide us and place the law in our
hearts, enabling us to pursue holiness and be alerted when we violate
one of God's standards.

The Church Age began at Pentecost, as described in Acts 2, and
will last until the Rapture described in 1 Thessalonians 4:13–17. The
church is not a denomination. It is not a group of buildings. The church

includes all people who have accepted Jesus as Savior and Lord, united by the indwelling Holy Spirit.

The Church Age will end with the Rapture of the church, when the seven-year tribulation prophesied by Daniel will occur.

Rapture

The Rapture of the church is revealed by Paul in 1 Thessalonians 4:13–17:

> Brothers and sisters, we do not want you to be uninformed about those who sleep in death, so that you do not grieve like the rest of mankind, who have no hope. For we believe that Jesus died and rose again, and so we believe that God will bring with Jesus those who have fallen asleep in him. According to the Lord's word, we tell you that we who are still alive, who are left until the coming of the Lord, will certainly not precede those who have fallen asleep. For the Lord himself will come down from heaven, with a loud command, with the voice of the archangel and with the trumpet call of God, and the dead in Christ will rise first. After that, we who are still alive and are left will be caught up together with them in the clouds to meet the Lord in the air. And so we will be with the Lord forever.

The word *rapture* comes from the Latin word *rapturo*, which is translated into English as "caught up" in verse 17. The Latin word *rapturo* was translated from the original Greek world *harpazo*, which meant snatched or taken away. All of this will occur very rapidly, "in the twinkling of an eye" as Paul describes in the following verse:

> Listen, I tell you a mystery: We will not all sleep, but we will all be changed—in a flash, in the twinkling of an eye, at the last trumpet. For the trumpet will sound, the dead will be raised imperishable, and we will be changed. (1 Corinthians 15:51–52)

At this time, all believers—those currently alive and those dead—will receive their resurrection bodies ("we shall be changed" referred to in the previous verse) and receive their rewards/crowns at the Bema Seat of Christ. This is not the Second Coming because Christ does not come down all the way to earth. Rather, believers will be caught up to Him in the clouds, similar to what happened to Jesus when He ascended to heaven forty days after the resurrection:

> After he said this, he was taken up before their very eyes, and a cloud hid him from their sight. They were looking intently up into the sky as he was going, when suddenly two men dressed in white stood beside them. "Men of Galilee," they said, "why do you stand here looking into the sky? This same Jesus, who has been taken from you into heaven, will come back in the same way you have seen him go into heaven." (Acts 1:9–11)

According to Messianic Jew and Bible teacher Amir Tsarfati, "The Rapture of the Church is the moment we will be with the Lord forever. From that moment on, we will never be away from Him physically, spiritually, or mentally."

Judgment (Bema) Seat of Christ

At the time of the Rapture, those who have claimed Jesus as Lord and Savior will participate in an awards ceremony called the Judgment Seat, or Bema Seat, of Christ.

> Therefore judge nothing before the appointed time; wait until the Lord comes. He will bring to light what is hidden in darkness and will expose the motives of the heart. At that time each will receive their praise from God. (1 Corinthians 4:5)

A bema seat in the ancient Olympics was the place where a judge would hand out rewards for finishing first, second, third, and so on.

The Greek word *bema* is translated "judgment seat" in English. These two verses address the Judgment Seat of Christ:

> For we must all appear before the judgment seat of Christ, so that each of us may receive what is due us for the things done while in the body, whether good or bad. (2 Corinthians 5:10)

> You, then, why do you judge your brother or sister? Or why do you treat them with contempt? For we will all stand before God's judgment seat. It is written: "As surely as I live,' says the Lord, 'every knee will bow before me; every tongue will acknowledge God.'" So then, each of us will give an account of ourselves to God. (Romans 14:10–12)

All believers will collectively stand before God's Judgment Seat. The only time it is possible for *all* believers to assemble together is after the Rapture.

Both good deeds, done for God's glory, and bad deeds, done for self-glorification, are exposed. However, the bad deeds are not punished. Rather, rewards are withheld (suffer loss), as explained in the following verse:

> If anyone builds on this foundation using gold, silver, costly stones, wood, hay or straw, their work will be shown for what it is, because the Day will bring it to light. It will be revealed with fire, and the fire will test the quality of each person's work. If what has been built survives, the builder will receive a reward. If it is burned up, the builder will suffer loss but yet will be saved—even though only as one escaping through the flames. (1 Corinthians 3:12–15)

Good deeds will result in rewards. Bad deeds will result in loss of rewards but not loss of salvation, which is fixed when we accept Christ as Savior.

The Bema Seat judgment is for believers. The Great White Throne Judgment, in contrast, is for unbelievers. The latter is for punishment for those who do not accept God's free gift of salvation through Jesus Christ. The Bema Seat judgment rewards believers for work done under the direction and influence of the Holy Spirit while on earth. Such work will be rewarded with crowns. Examples of work meriting a reward includes discipling others, overcoming sin, exerting self-discipline, manifesting the fruit of the Spirit, and so on. More about this in chapter 7.

Tribulation

After the church (all believers) is taken from the earth and united with Jesus during the Rapture, a seven-year period called the tribulation will take place. The church does not have to go through this, as the following verse suggests:

> For God did not appoint us to suffer wrath but to receive salvation through our Lord Jesus Christ. (1 Thessalonians 5:9)

The word *tribulation* appears in the King James Version of the Bible and is translated as "distress" in the New International Version.

> For then there will be great distress, unequaled from the beginning of the world until now—and never to be equaled again. (Matthew 24:21)

> Immediately after the distress of those days 'the sun will be darkened, and the moon will not give its light; the stars will fall from the sky, and the heavenly bodies will be shaken.' (Matthew 24:29)

In other parts of the Bible, it is referred to as the "day of the Lord" (Isaiah 13:6) and "time of trouble for Jacob" (Jeremiah 30:7). or "time of distress" (Daniel 12:1).

This seven-year period is prophesied in the following verse, where it refers to the tribulation period as "one seven:"

> He will confirm a covenant with many for one "seven."
> In the middle of the "seven" he will put an end to
> sacrifice and offering. And at the temple he will set up
> an abomination that causes desolation, until the end
> that is decreed is poured out on him. (Daniel 9:27)

The seven represents seven years. We derive this from verses 25 and 26 where a length of time of sixty-nine sevens (69 x 7 = 483) was predicted to elapse between the decree to rebuild Jerusalem and the crucifixion of a Savior. Four hundred and eighty-three years did actually elapse, so each seven was seven years.

During this period, the person called the Antichrist (1 John 2:18), also referred to as the "man of lawlessness" (2 Thessalonians 2:3), "beast" (Revelation 13:1), and the "He" of Daniel 9:27 above, will come into power and sign a covenant with Israel (Daniel 9:27). During this seven-year period, there will be terrible wars, famines, plagues, and natural disasters caused by God's wrath against sin.

During the middle of the tribulation (three and a half years), the Antichrist will break the covenant with Israel and will launch an attack on Jerusalem to wipe out the Jews, resulting in the battle of Armageddon.

> Then they gathered the kings together to the place that
> in Hebrew is called Armageddon. (Revelation 16:16)

Only the Second Coming of Jesus will prevent the entire population of the earth from being wiped out.

Second Coming of Jesus

The first coming of Jesus was as a Savior to die for the sins of humankind. He died and rose again so that sinful people can be admitted into a holy God's presence, provided those people claim the gift that Jesus gave them and rely on that gift alone for their salvation. This was in fulfilment of numerous prophecies, some of which we described in chapter 2. However, there were several prophecies that as yet are unfulfilled, such as the following:

> For to us a child is born, to us a son is given, and the government will be on his shoulders. And he will be called Wonderful Counselor, Mighty God, Everlasting Father, Prince of Peace. Of the greatness of his government and peace there will be no end. He will reign on David's throne and over his kingdom, establishing and upholding it with justice and righteousness from that time on and forever. The zeal of the LORD Almighty will accomplish this. (Isaiah 9:6–7)

Jesus has not yet established a government on earth.

> I will gather all the nations to Jerusalem to fight against it; the city will be captured, the houses ransacked, and the women raped. Half of the city will go into exile, but the rest of the people will not be taken from the city. Then the LORD will go out and fight against those nations, as he fights on a day of battle. On that day his feet will stand on the Mount of Olives, east of Jerusalem, and the Mount of Olives will be split in two from east to west, forming a great valley, with half of the mountain moving north and half moving south. (Zechariah 14:2–4)

This hasn't occurred yet either; Jesus has not set his feet on the Mount of Olives, nor has the Mount of Olives split. These unfulfilled prophecies will be satisfied at Jesus's Second Coming as Conquering King, when he arrives with the armies of heaven.

> Then will appear the sign of the Son of Man in heaven. And then all the peoples of the earth will mourn when they see the Son of Man coming on the clouds of heaven, with power and great glory. (Matthew 24:30)

71

While we wait for the blessed hope—the appearing of the glory of our great God and Savior, Jesus Christ. (Titus 2:13)

"Look, he is coming with the clouds," and "every eye will see him, even those who pierced him"; and all peoples on earth "will mourn because of him." So shall it be! Amen. (Revelation 1:7)

A more detailed description of Jesus's Second Coming is found in the following verses:

I saw heaven standing open and there before me was a white horse, whose rider is called Faithful and True. With justice he judges and wages war. His eyes are like blazing fire, and on his head are many crowns. He has a name written on him that no one knows but he himself. He is dressed in a robe dipped in blood, and his name is the Word of God. The armies of heaven were following him, riding on white horses and dressed in fine linen, white and clean. Coming out of his mouth is a sharp sword with which to strike down the nations. "He will rule them with an iron scepter." He treads the winepress of the fury of the wrath of God Almighty. On his robe and on his thigh he has this name written: KING OF KINGS AND LORD OF LORDS. (Revelation 19:11–16)

This heavenly warrior is Jesus. He is referred to as the Word of God in the book of John:

In the beginning was the Word, and the Word was with God, and the Word was God. (John 1:1)

The Word became flesh and made his dwelling among us. We have seen his glory, the glory of the one and only Son, who came from the Father, full of grace and truth. (John 1:14)

Millennial Reign

Once Jesus defeats the armies of Armageddon, He will begin His millennial reign, which will last one thousand years on earth. It will be a time of peace, joy, comfort, holiness, truth, and the knowledge of God. Christ will rule as king from Jerusalem.

> I saw thrones on which were seated those who had been given authority to judge. And I saw the souls of those who had been beheaded because of their testimony about Jesus and because of the word of God. They had not worshiped the beast or its image and had not received its mark on their foreheads or their hands. They came to life and reigned with Christ a thousand years. (Revelation 20:4)

Great White Throne Judgment

At the end of the millennial reign of Jesus, Satan, who has been bound one thousand years, will be released for a brief period. He will deceive people again and cause one more rebellion against the Lord but will be quickly defeated by the Lord, as described here:

> When the thousand years are over, Satan will be released from his prison and will go out to deceive the nations in the four corners of the earth—Gog and Magog—and to gather them for battle. In number they are like the sand on the seashore. They marched across the breadth of the earth and surrounded the camp of God's people, the city he loves. But fire came down from heaven and devoured them. And the devil, who deceived them, was thrown into the lake of burning sulfur, where the beast and the false prophet had been thrown. They will be tormented day and night for ever and ever. (Revelation 20:7–10)

The final judgment of all unbelievers is called the Great White Throne Judgment. It is described in the following verse: Revelation 20:11-13.

> Then I saw a great white throne and him who was seated on it. The earth and the heavens fled from his presence, and there was no place for them. And I saw the dead, great and small, standing before the throne, and books were opened. Another book was opened, which is the book of life. The dead were judged according to what they had done as recorded in the books. The sea gave up the dead that were in it, and death and Hades gave up the dead that were in them, and each person was judged according to what they had done.

All people will appear in a courtroom setting before God, the divine judge. Each sinner comes before the bar of God. Books are opened, and nonbelievers are judged according to their works, but of course works will not save them. The fact that "each person was judged according to what they had done" could indicate that there are different degrees of punishment in hell.

It could also indicate a trial proceeding where the sinner represents himself. All of the evidence is disclosed, including all of the thoughts, words and deeds of commission and omission; all of the choices a person made over his life; and all of the chances he had to accept Jesus as Savior but didn't. It will eliminate any doubt that the person is guilty. The evidence will be overwhelming.

Another book, called the Book of Life is also opened. The Book of Life is mentioned throughout the Bible. An Old Testament example is what the prophet Daniel wrote in the 600s BC:

> At that time Michael, the great prince who protects your people, will arise. There will be a time of distress such as has not happened from the beginning of nations until then. But at that time your people—everyone whose

name is found written in the book—will be delivered. (Daniel 12:1)

A later New Testament example is what Paul wrote in the AD 60s:

> Yes, and I ask you, my true companion, help these women since they have contended at my side in the cause of the gospel, along with Clement and the rest of my co-workers, whose names are in the book of life. (Philippians 4:3)

All believers whose names are written in the Book of Life are represented by a defense attorney, Jesus Christ himself.

> My dear children, I write this to you so that you will not sin. But if anybody does sin, we have an advocate with the Father—Jesus Christ, the Righteous One. (1 John 2:1)

Those whose names are written in the Book of Life are spared and excluded from the Great White Throne Judgment.

Lake of Fire

All people whose names are not written in the Book of Life will be condemned and thrown into the Lake of Fire:

> Then death and Hades were thrown into the lake of fire. The lake of fire is the second death. Anyone whose name was not found written in the book of life was thrown into the lake of fire. (Revelation 20:14–15)

New Heaven and New Earth

Once all unsaved sinners and Satan and his demons are cast into the Lake of Fire, never to return, God will have finalized the roster of those who will live with Him for eternity. At this time, He will refurbish the destination where those people will live. It is the greatest tear-down-and-rebuild project in history! God will demolish the old universe and restore it to the pristine condition He had in mind when He originally created it. This was prophesied by Isaiah in the 700s BC:

> See, I will create new heavens and a new earth. The former things will not be remembered, nor will they come to mind. (Isaiah 65:17)

> "As the new heavens and the new earth that I make will endure before me," declares the Lord, "so will your name and descendants endure." (Isaiah 66:22)

This was also prophesied by the apostle Peter in the AD 60s:

> But the day of the Lord will come like a thief. The heavens will disappear with a roar; the elements will be destroyed by fire, and the earth and everything done in it will be laid bare. Since everything will be destroyed in this way, what kind of people ought you to be? You ought to live holy and godly lives as you look forward to the day of God and speed its coming. That day will bring about the destruction of the heavens by fire, and the elements will melt in the heat. But in keeping with his promise we are looking forward to a new heaven and a new earth, where righteousness dwells. (2 Peter 3:10–13)

Rather than God destroying the universe and creating something new, Luke writes that God will restore what He originally created:

> Heaven must receive him until the time comes for God to restore everything, as he promised long ago through his holy prophets. (Acts 3:21)

The apostle John, in the vision he received on the island of Patmos around AD 90 and recorded in the book of Revelation, describes his vision about the new heaven and new earth:

> Then I saw "a new heaven and a new earth," for the first heaven and the first earth had passed away, and there was no longer any sea. I saw the Holy City, the new Jerusalem, coming down out of heaven from God, prepared as a bride beautifully dressed for her husband. And I heard a loud voice from the throne saying, "Look! God's dwelling place is now among the people, and he will dwell with them. They will be his people, and God himself will be with them and be their God. 'He will wipe every tear from their eyes. There will be no more death' or mourning or crying or pain, for the old order of things has passed away." (Revelation 21:1–4)

This is ultimately the final goal, the new heaven and new earth, where we will reign with Jesus forever. No more lies and half-truths, fake news, perversion, pain, frustration, and sorrow. Only the knowledge of God, purity, comfort, purpose, and joy.

You Are Here

There is compelling evidence that we are close to the end-times. Just a sample of this evidence is the following:

- Israel has been restored as a country.
- An alliance of prophesied countries hostile to Israel has been formed.
- Third temple preparations have been made.
- Technology for the mark of the beast has been developed.

Israel has been restored as a country. In 1948, for the first time since AD 70, Israel was again a country. This was prophesied by Ezekiel in the 500s BC:

> And say to them, "This is what the Sovereign LORD says: 'I will take the Israelites out of the nations where they have gone. I will gather them from all around and bring them back into their own land.'" (Ezekiel 37:21)

An alliance of prophesied countries hostile to Israel has been formed. Ezekiel also prophesied that specific countries will ally and attack Israel.

> The word of the Lord came to me: "Son of man, set your face against Gog, of the land of Magog, the chief prince of Meshek and Tubal; prophesy against him and say: 'This is what the Sovereign Lord says: I am against you, Gog, chief prince of Meshek and Tubal. I will turn you around, put hooks in your jaws and bring you out with your whole army—your horses, your horsemen fully armed, and a great horde with large and small shields, all of them brandishing their swords. Persia, Cush and Put will be with them, all with shields and helmets, also Gomer with all its troops, and Beth Togarmah from the far north with all its troops—the many nations with you.'" (Ezekiel 38:1–6)

For the first time in history, we are witnessing these countries aligning themselves against Israel. Each is listed below:

- Magog is Russia.
- Meshech is Moscow. Classical Greek writers called the people of Meshech the "Moschoi."
- Tubal is named after the Tobol River, on which is situated the city of Tobolsk, once Russia's Asian capital.
- Persia is Iran.
- Cush is Sudan/Ethiopia.
- Put is Libya/Algeria.
- Gomer is central Turkey.
- Beth Togarmah is eastern Turkey.

Russia, Iran, and Turkey have entered into a secret alliance, symbolized by a photo of Presidents Hassan Rouhani of Iran, Tayyip Erdogan of Turkey, and Vladimir Putin of Russia clasping hands in a meeting in Ankara Turkey on April 4, 2018.[13] This has never happened before.

Third temple preparations have been made. There must be a temple on the Temple Mount, where the Dome of the Rock, an Islamic mosque, now sits. Prophecies include a Jewish temple, so one must be rebuilt. The following Bible verse and prophecy mentions "God's temple:"

> Don't let anyone deceive you in any way, for that day will not come until the rebellion occurs and the man of lawlessness is revealed, the man doomed to destruction. He will oppose and will exalt himself over everything that is called God or is worshiped, so that he sets himself up in God's temple, proclaiming himself to be God. (2 Thessalonians 2:3–4)

Before a temple is rebuilt, plans are underway to furnish it and resume sacrifices. For example, on Hanukah December 10, 2018, an activist group in Israel built and dedicated the altar for the new temple.[14] The Temple Institute imported frozen embryos and implanted them in Israeli cows, and an entirely red calf was born (one with no more than two nonred hairs on its body).[15] This was done to fulfil the following:

> The Lord said to Moses and Aaron: "This is a requirement of the law that the Lord has commanded: Tell the Israelites to bring you a red heifer without defect or blemish and that has never been under a yoke. Give it to Eleazar the priest; it is to be taken outside the camp and slaughtered in his presence. (Numbers 19:1–3)

Technology for the mark of the beast has been developed. The book of Revelation states that the Antichrist (beast) will require a mark on the right hands or foreheads of his subjects that will enable them to purchase and sell goods and services:

> It [beast] also forced all people, great and small, rich
> and poor, free and slave, to receive a mark on their right
> hands or on their foreheads, so that they could not buy
> or sell unless they had the mark, which is the name
> of the beast or the number of its name. (Revelation
> 13:16-17)

This technology is already developed and has been used in Sweden since 2015. A tiny microchip, the size of a grain of rice, is inserted under the skin, precluding the need to carry keys, credit cards, and train tickets. The Swedes are very active in microchipping. Three thousand Swedes had microchips injected into their hands in 2018. Passengers of Sweden's national railway use the implanted chips to board the trains after making reservations online. Conductors merely scan passengers' hands when they board.[16]

The end-times are drawing near, maybe nearer than anyone realizes. Although we may not be close to dying, we still may be close to entering heaven via the Rapture. Now is the time to earn rewards in heaven. Now is the time to prepare.

6

Crowns and Rewards to Train For

Athletes must compete to qualify for the Olympic team every four years. If they make the team, they can earn gold, silver, or bronze medals at the Olympic games. They train hard and keep their eyes on the prize.

To qualify for the team going to heaven, we don't compete and can't earn a spot. All we can do is humbly accept the payment that Jesus made on the cross for our sins, the only acceptable price of admission to God's kingdom. Once we are born again, our sins are forgiven, we have assurance we will go to heaven, we are viewed by God as saints, we are adopted into God's family, and we are indwelt by the Holy Spirit. We now live under God's authority and seek to please God with the Holy Spirit's guidance.

Like the Olympics, there are crowns and rewards in heaven, and this chapter reveals what they are. Jesus stated,

> "Do not store up for yourselves treasures on earth, where moths and vermin destroy, and where thieves break in and steal. But store up for yourselves treasures in heaven, where moths and vermin do not destroy, and where thieves do not break in and steal. For where your treasure is, there your heart will be also." (Matthew 6:19–21)

Jesus instructs us not to store up treasure on earth, which is perishable, but to store up treasure in heaven, which is imperishable. Paul writes about using gold, silver, and costly stones to build on Christ's foundation:

> By the grace God has given me, I laid a foundation as a wise builder, and someone else is building on it. But each one should build with care. For no one can lay any foundation other than the one already laid, which is Jesus Christ. If anyone builds on this foundation using gold, silver, costly stones, wood, hay or straw, their work will be shown for what it is, because the Day will bring it to light. It will be revealed with fire, and the fire will

test the quality of each person's work. If what has been built survives, the builder will receive a reward. If it is burned up, the builder will suffer loss but yet will be saved—even though only as one escaping through the flames. (1 Corinthians 3:10–15)

So which type of construction work builds on Christ's foundation? Paul writes that there are two types of workers: one who plants (evangelizes) by sharing the Gospel message, and one who waters (disciples) by teaching, reproving, and encouraging.

The one who plants and the one who waters have one purpose, and they will each be rewarded according to their own labor. (1 Corinthians 3:8)

The one purpose that unites the two workers is to draw people to Christ. If workers spread worldly wisdom that is perishable, it is wood, hay, or straw that will burn up. If workers spread godly wisdom from the Bible, it is like gold, silver, and costly stones that will last.

Motivation

Our motive to seek crowns and rewards in heaven is important, however. The "why" is important. To push through the inevitable obstacles and frustrations of life, we must fully understand *why* we are trying to accomplish something. Is it status we are seeking? Men's approval? Or, is our motive to please God?

In Jeremiah, it states that God knows our motives. If they are selfish, we can expect to earn little treasure in heaven.

"I the Lord search the heart and examine the mind, to reward each person according to their conduct, according to what their deeds deserve." (Jeremiah 17:10)

Paul says we should lead our lives to please the Lord. We all must appear before Christ to receive what we are due for our thoughts, words, and actions while on earth.

So we make it our goal to please him, whether we are at home in the body or away from it. For we must all appear before the judgment seat of Christ, so that each of us may receive what is due us for the things done while in the body, whether good or bad. (2 Corinthians 5:9–10)

To please God requires sufficient faith to earnestly seek Him:

And without faith it is impossible to please God, because anyone who comes to him must believe that he exists and that he rewards those who earnestly seek him. (Hebrews 11:6)

To please God means to obey His commandments:

The fear of the Lord is pure, enduring forever. The decrees of the Lord are firm, and all of them are righteous. They are more precious than gold, than much pure gold; they are sweeter than honey, than honey from the honeycomb. By them your servant is warned; in keeping them there is great reward. (Psalm 19:9-11)

For us to produce the works on earth that will lead to rewards in heaven, we must please God and obey His commandments. Therefore, we should heed what Jesus said was the most important commandments to obey:

Hearing that Jesus had silenced the Sadducees, the Pharisees got together. One of them, an expert in the law, tested him with this question: "Teacher, which is the greatest commandment in the Law?" Jesus replied: "'Love the Lord your God with all your heart and with all your soul and with all your mind.' This is the first and greatest commandment. And the second is like it: 'Love your neighbor as yourself.' All the Law and

the Prophets hang on these two commandments."
(Matthew 22:34–40)

Jesus said we must love God with all of our heart, soul, and mind and love our neighbor as ourselves. This is our motivation. To earn crowns and rewards in heaven should be a labor of love for God.

Crowns and Rewards

So then, what are the crowns and rewards we can accumulate in heaven? The New Testament describes five crowns that we can earn on earth to receive in heaven:

1. Crown of righteousness: yearning for Jesus's return and reign.
2. Soul-winner's crown: leading others to Christ.
3. Crown of life: persevering through persecution with love.
4. Crown of glory: modeling Christian leadership.
5. Crown of victory: disciplining the mind by praying and studying the Bible.

1. Crown of Righteousness

You can earn the crown of righteousness by yearning for Jesus's return and reign.

> Now there is in store for me the crown of righteousness, which the Lord, the righteous Judge, will award to me on that day—and not only to me, but also to all who have longed for his appearing. (2 Timothy 4:8)

You will yearn for Christ's return only if you know you are saved. Do you believe that Christ paid the penalty for your sin by dying on the cross and rising from the dead? Do you repent of your sins and cry out to Jesus for forgiveness? If so, you have assurance of salvation. You are depending exclusively on God's grace, not your works or merit.

You will yearn for Christ's return only if you are tired of the unrighteousness of this world and recognize that this world is not your home. A believer's citizenship is in heaven. On earth, we are just passing through.

You will yearn for Christ's return only if you long for a holy place to live, for the restoration of the Garden of Eden, and for the love, peace and joy promised in heaven.

Anyone who seeks to lead a holy life, to obey God's commandments, and to please God, will grieve over the state of the world today. Wickedness is encouraged and applauded, not God's decrees. There is so much evil in the world today, such as sexual sin, violence, and drugs. How can you not yearn for Jesus to return and make all things right, restoring holiness to the earth?

2. Soul-Winner's Crown

You can earn the soul winner's crown by leading others to Christ.

> For what is our hope, our joy, or the crown in which
> we will glory in the presence of our Lord Jesus when he
> comes? Is it not you? Indeed, you are our glory and joy.
> (1 Thessalonians 2:19–20)

You lead a person to Christ by making a clear concise presentation of the gospel and praying that it is received. When Paul wrote to the church in Thessalonica, he revealed that he cared for the people in the church like a mother caring for her children, sharing the Gospel and his life with them.

> Instead, we were like young children among you. Just as
> a nursing mother cares for her children, so we cared for
> you. Because we loved you so much, we were delighted
> to share with you not only the gospel of God but our
> lives as well. (1 Thessalonians 2:7–8)

Farther down in the letter, he reveals that he dealt with the people in the Thessalonica church as a father would with his own children, by encouraging, comforting, and urging them to live righteous lives pleasing to God.

> For you know that we dealt with each of you as a father deals with his own children, encouraging, comforting and urging you to live lives worthy of God, who calls you into his kingdom and glory. (1 Thessalonians 2:11–12)

There can be no greater reward in heaven than to see a person who is there because you shared the gospel.

3. Crown of Life

You can earn the crown of life by persevering through persecution with love.

> Blessed is the one who perseveres under trial because, having stood the test, that person will receive the crown of life that the Lord has promised to those who love him. (James 1:12)

Following God's decrees, speaking the truth of God's Word, and condemning wickedness in the world will result in persecution. We see that happening on social media, the radio, and television. People are condemned for saying homosexual sex is sin, sex-change operations are not ordained by God, abortion is killing a baby in the womb, Jesus is the only way to heaven, and so on. Jesus said to rejoice and be glad when persecution occurs, for great is your reward in heaven.

> "Blessed are you when people insult you, persecute you and falsely say all kinds of evil against you because of me. Rejoice and be glad, because great is your reward in heaven, for in the same way they persecuted the prophets who were before you." (Matthew 5:11–12)

What does persecution look like? Notice what Jesus says: people will hate and insult you. They will call you evil and a hater. They will exclude you.

> "Blessed are you when people hate you, when they exclude you and insult you and reject your name as evil,

because of the Son of Man. Rejoice in that day and leap for joy, because great is your reward in heaven. For that is how their ancestors treated the prophets." (Luke 6:22–23)

There is worse persecution though. In Hebrews, the author reports that people had their property confiscated. We see that today. Baker Jack Phillips, who refused to create a custom-made cake celebrating a gay marriage and another cake celebrating a sex change, was persecuted, fined by the Colorado Equal Rights Commission, and lost 40 percent of his business.[17] Florist and grandmother Barronelle Stutzman, who refused to create a custom-made floral arrangement for a gay wedding, was fined by the Washington Equal Rights Commission and could lose her life savings and home.[18]

Remember those earlier days after you had received the light, when you endured in a great conflict full of suffering. Sometimes you were publicly exposed to insult and persecution; at other times you stood side by side with those who were so treated. You suffered along with those in prison and joyfully accepted the confiscation of your property, because you knew that you yourselves had better and lasting possessions. So do not throw away your confidence; it will be richly rewarded. (Hebrews 10:32–35)

There are also those who have been persecuted and lost their lives, such as the twenty Coptic Christians from Egypt and one believer from Ghana, beheaded by ISIS on the shores of the Mediterranean in Libya.[19]

Jesus further instructs that we should love our enemies and pray for those who persecute us.

"You have heard that it was said, 'Love your neighbor and hate your enemy.' But I tell you, love your enemies and pray for those who persecute you, that you may be children of your Father in heaven. He causes his sun to rise on the evil and the good, and sends rain on the righteous and the unrighteous. If you love those who love you, what reward will you get? Are not even the tax collectors doing that? And if you greet only your own people, what are you doing more than others? Do not even pagans do that? (Matthew 5:43–47)

The message in Proverbs 25:21-22 is similar:

If your enemy is hungry, give him food to eat; if he is thirsty, give him water to drink. In doing this, you will heap burning coals on his head, and the Lord will reward you.

When persecuted for Jesus's sake and praying for your persecutors, you can earn the crown of life.

4. Crown of Glory

You can earn the crown of glory by modeling Christian leadership.

Be shepherds of God's flock that is under your care, watching over them—not because you must, but because you are willing, as God wants you to be; not pursuing dishonest gain, but eager to serve; not lording it over those entrusted to you, but being examples to the flock. And when the Chief Shepherd appears, you will receive the crown of glory that will never fade away. (1 Peter 5:2–4)

The role of a leader in church is important. The apostle Paul lists the qualities of a church leader in Titus 1:6–9:

An elder must be blameless, faithful to his wife, a man whose children believe and are not open to the charge of being wild and disobedient. Since an overseer manages God's household, he must be blameless— not overbearing, not quick-tempered, not given to drunkenness, not violent, not pursuing dishonest gain. Rather, he must be hospitable, one who loves what is good, who is self-controlled, upright, holy and disciplined. He must hold firmly to the trustworthy message as it has been taught, so that he can encourage others by sound doctrine and refute those who oppose it.

Those leaders who volunteer willingly and not by compulsion, lead with humility and by example, and are even-tempered, honest, and faithful can earn the crown of glory.

5. Crown of Victory

You can earn the crown of victory by disciplining your mind by praying and studying the Bible.

Do you not know that in a race all the runners run, but only one gets the prize? Run in such a way as to get the prize. Everyone who competes in the games goes into strict training. They do it to get a crown that will not last, but we do it to get a crown that will last forever. (1 Corinthians 9:24–25)

Olympic athletes are focused and self-disciplined. Their strict training focuses on activities that will achieve their goals and rejects activities that are diversions. Their self-discipline follows a tailored exercise program and diet.

To win the crown of victory we also must be self-disciplined. We focus on activities that will earn the crown, such as praying and studying the Bible. These activities train our spiritual muscles.

Through self-discipline, Olympic athletes build muscle, reduce fat, and improve performance. Through prayer and Bible study, Christians build spiritual muscle, reduce selfish desire and behavior dishonoring to God, and improve spiritual gifts used in ministry. Through self-discipline, Christians can earn the crown of victory and more effectively build on Christ's foundation with gold, silver, and costly stones.

Crowns Are Earned for Responsible Positions in Heaven

So what is the use of crowns in heaven? Randy Alcorn, in his book *Heaven*, states, "Because crowns are the primary symbol of ruling, every mention of crowns as rewards is a reference to our ruling with Christ."[20] Therefore, it appears that crowns are related to positions of responsibility given in heaven to rule and to judge.

We are told that crowns were given to the elders in heaven who laid their crowns before Christ in recognition of his glory, honor, and power.

> The twenty-four elders fall down before him who sits on the throne and worship him who lives for ever and ever. They lay their crowns before the throne and say: "You are worthy, our Lord and God, to receive glory and honor and power, for you created all things, and by your will they were created and have their being." (Revelation 4:10–11)

Perhaps the crowns are exchanged for positions in Jesus's kingdom as the parable of the ten minas, described in Luke 19:11–26, would imply. In this parable, a man of noble birth is sent to a distant country to be appointed king and to return at a later date. Before leaving, he calls ten of his servants, giving each ten minas to invest. When the nobleman returns, the first servant reveals that he has earned ten additional minas.

> "Well done, my good servant!" his master replied. "Because you have been trustworthy in a very small matter, take charge of ten cities." (Luke 19:17)

The second servant has earned five minas.

> His master answered, "You take charge of five cities." (Luke 19:19)

The last servant hid the original minas given and didn't earn anything.

His master replied, "I will judge you by your own words, you wicked servant! You knew, did you, that I am a hard man, taking out what I did not put in, and reaping what I did not sow? Why then didn't you put my money on deposit, so that when I came back, I could have collected it with interest?" Then he said to those standing by, "Take his mina away from him and give it to the one who has ten minas." (Luke 19:22–24)

In this parable, the master is Jesus. He goes to another country, which represents heaven. We are the servants. We are entrusted with spiritual gifts and are expected to use them to build on Christ's foundation with gold, silver, and valuable stones, which are imperishable works. Our reward is responsibility, to take charge of things in heaven, perhaps even whole cities there.

For some people, being in charge of something, particularly cities in heaven, is threatening and does not seem like much of a reward. Randy Alcorn assures them that:

Service is a reward, not a punishment. This idea is foreign to people who dislike their work and only put up with it until retirement. We think that faithful work should be rewarded by a vacation for the rest of our lives. But God offers us something very different: more work, more responsibilities, increased opportunities, along with greater abilities, resources, wisdom, and empowerment. We will have sharp minds, strong bodies, clear purpose, and unabated joy. The more we serve Christ now, the greater capacity will be to serve him in Heaven.[21]

What does "take charge of things" entail? The New Testament mentions ruling and judging.

Ruling

> His master replied, "Well done, good and faithful servant! You have been faithful with a few things; I will put you in charge of many things. Come and share your master's happiness!" (Matthew 25:23)

> If we endure, we will also reign with him. If we disown him, he will also disown us. (2 Timothy 2:12)

Judging

> Or do you not know that the Lord's people will judge the world? And if you are to judge the world, are you not competent to judge trivial cases? Do you not know that we will judge angels? How much more the things of this life! (1 Corinthians 6:2–3)

> And I confer on you a kingdom, just as my Father conferred one on me, so that you may eat and drink at my table in my kingdom and sit on thrones, judging the twelve tribes of Israel. (Luke 22:29–30)

We know that our destination is heaven. We know that we can receive rewards in heaven by working on the foundation of Jesus, advancing God's kingdom, sharing the Gospel, and ministering to others while we live on earth. We know that we can receive crowns and be granted responsibilities in heaven. Let's now get to work and formulate a plan, which is the subject of the next chapter.

7

A Plan to Earn Crowns and Rewards in Heaven

In this chapter, we will describe how to earn crowns and rewards by employing spiritual gifts and SMART goals. God has equipped us with special abilities to serve Him, minister to the church, and earn rewards in heaven. These special abilities are called spiritual gifts.

We should keep in mind that the crowns and rewards will accrue to us if we work to advance God's kingdom.

> But seek first his kingdom and his righteousness, and all these things will be given to you as well. (Matthew 6:33)

The motivation to earn crowns and rewards is important. It should not be for self-promotion or approval from others.

> Be careful not to practice your righteousness in front of others to be seen by them. If you do, you will have no reward from your Father in heaven. (Matthew 6:1)

> On the contrary, we speak as those approved by God to be entrusted with the gospel. We are not trying to please people but God, who tests our hearts. (1 Thessalonians 2:4)

Our motivation should be to love God and to love our neighbor as ourselves. We serve because we are grateful to Jesus for what He did for us on the cross. Otherwise, we could not even go to heaven. The crowns are a by-product of living a life obedient to God and responding to prompts of the Holy Spirit to advance God's kingdom. By pleasing God and obeying Him, the crowns and rewards will come naturally.

Routine Christian Service Not Requiring Spiritual Gifts

Before we get to the discussion of spiritual gifts, there are certain duties we as Christians are required to do that are similar to, but don't require, spiritual gifts. We are *all* commanded to do the following, irrespective of our spiritual gifts:

- We are to share the Gospel, contained in the Great Commission below.

   Therefore go and make disciples of all nations, baptizing them in the name of the Father and of the Son and of the Holy Spirit. (Matthew 28:19)

- We are to give tithes and offerings to the church and to the needy.

   Each of you should give what you have decided in your heart to give, not reluctantly or under compulsion, for God loves a cheerful giver. (2 Corinthians 9:7)

- We are to be hospitable to others.

   Share with the Lord's people who are in need. Practice hospitality. (Romans 12:13)

These are just a few of the routine acts we should do to lead the Christian life. Now we will turn our attention to spiritual gifts.

Spiritual Gifts

Pursuing a ministry while on life's journey is most productive if we use our spiritual gifts. Employing our spiritual gifts is like taking the scenic route on a vacation. It provides the most satisfying and enjoyable experience.

Each born-again believer is given at least one spiritual gift by the Holy Spirit at the moment of conversion. The Holy Spirit bestows spiritual gifts to members of the church to enable the church to carry out its mission to make disciples, glorify Christ, and build up its people.

A spiritual gift is different from a natural talent. Some people are naturally artistic or mechanical, for example. A spiritual gift could enhance the natural talent to help the church carry out its mission, or the spiritual gift could be a new talent. If believers faithfully use the original gift provided by the Holy Spirit, the Holy Spirit may give additional spiritual gifts as ministry needs arise. People cannot choose their gift, but if we are faithful with the gift(s) already given, we can pray for another, and the Holy Spirit will bestow as He sees fit.

Spiritual gifts come to us in the rough. Believers must employ their gift in ministry to develop the gift, just as practicing anything makes you more proficient. If believers do not use and develop their gift, they can lose it and be rebuked by the Lord.

There are multiple spiritual gifts listed in the Bible. The verses that address spiritual gifts are Romans 12:6–8; 1 Corinthians 12:8–10, 28–30; and Ephesians 4:11. We will concentrate on the seven gifts listed in Romans 12:6–8. Some theologians believe that certain spiritual gifts listed in 1 Corinthians 12 and Ephesians 4 were given only to the original apostles or are given only on special occasions by the Holy Spirit.

> We have different gifts, according to the grace given to each of us. If your gift is prophesying, then prophesy in accordance with your faith; if it is serving, then serve; if it is teaching, then teach; if it is to encourage, then give encouragement; if it is giving, then give generously; if it is to lead, do it diligently; if it is to show mercy, do it cheerfully. (Romans 12:6–8)

The discussion of the seven gifts below is taken from Charles F. Stanley's book, *Ministering Through Spiritual Gifts: Recognize Your Personal Gifts and Use Them to Further the Kingdom*[22] and John MacArthur's online Spiritual Gifts Study Guide[23] at the Grace to You website.

- Prophecy
- Service
- Teaching
- Encouragement
- Giving
- Leadership
- Mercy

We will provide some examples of SMART goals for each spiritual gift. SMART goals are written goals that are specific, measurable, achievable, realistic, and timely (with a finish date). SMART goals are effective because they are clear and specific and hold you accountable to do a specific action by a specific date.

Prophecy

Definition: People with the gift of prophecy publicly proclaim God's word. They are prompted by the Holy Spirit to proclaim the truth of the Bible to edify, exhort, and warn the church. They instruct the church to improve its morals and strengthen its faith. They confront—without worrying about personal consequences—evil, hypocrisy, error, and deceit and defend God's nature, word, and church.

Old Testament prophets delivered messages from God, acting as a mediator between the people and God. Today, Jesus is our mediator, and there is a strict warning in Revelation 22:18-19 against adding anything to Scripture. There is also a warning in Matthew 7:15 about the prevalence of false prophets during the last days.

Prophecy can include foretelling (predicting the future) or forthtelling, (proclaiming God's word and applying it to a need or situation). Some Christians believe that the foretelling of the prophets in the Old and New Testaments has ceased. Others believe it still exists. In its extreme form, Paul describes prophecy in 1 Corinthians 13:2 as understanding all mysteries and knowledge.

Examples: Speaks in public proclaiming God's word to edify, exhort, or warn the church.

SMART Goal Examples:

- By June 30, I will ask my church leaders if I may warn the church about a current issue.
- Beginning today and continuing for two months, I will study the Bible and prepare an article for some online forum that relates the truth of the Bible to a current issue.
- By June 30 I will ask an organization if I can proclaim God's word about a current event or issue in the world.

Service

Definition: People with the gift of service perform many different types of work—no matter if it is menial—to help others in ministry. They are often project oriented, enjoy working with their hands, are alert to the needs of others, and feel satisfied by lightening the load of other people to enable them to more fully pursue their ministry calling. Service is the most needed and common gift.

Examples: Cleans the church or does repair work, greets on Sundays or works in the nursery, counts offerings, drives shut-ins to church, makes coffee in the morning.

SMART Goal Examples:

- By June 30, I will contact a local Christian ministry to see if there are any tasks or projects that I can volunteer for.
- By June 30, I will select and volunteer for a weekly ministry at church, such as serving at the information desk, joining the landscaping crew, or directing traffic after the Sunday service.
- I will complete one short-term missionary trip by August 31 to help in any way needed.

Teaching

Definition: People with the gift of teaching can systematically teach the truth of God's word. They are able to explain what the Bible means and how to apply biblical principles to our lives. Teachers have a strong desire to convey the lessons of the Bible in an easy-to-understand and step-by-step manner. They use appropriate vocabulary for the listener and research topics extensively.

Examples: Teaches adult or youth Bible classes, writes books about scriptural topics, develops courses and prepares the supporting materials, homeschools children.

SMART Goal Examples:

- By June 30, I will ask if I can contribute a series of articles on a scriptural topic to the church website or newsletter.
- By June 30, I will ask the church if there is a class I can teach, either for children or adults.

- Beginning June 1, for three months I will study a book or topic in the Bible and create a series of presentations I can give to a Sunday school class.

Encouragement

Definition: People with the gift of encouragement exhort, motivate, and strengthen others to overcome problems, grow in their faith, and reach their God-given potential. By communicating biblical truth, an encourager dissuades people from committing sinful acts or helps them recover from past mistakes. This can occur through prophesying, teaching, counseling, or conversation. Encouragers are people persons who use God's wisdom to discern another person's problem or potential.

Examples: Counsels adults or mentors youth by encouraging them with scripture and helping them apply scripture to their lives.

SMART Goal Examples:

- By June 30, I will find three biblical counseling courses I can take or books I can read and will choose one to complete by August 31.
- By June 30, I will inquire at my church if there are any youth or young adults who need mentoring or counseling, will pick one, and set up a weekly/biweekly/monthly time to meet for the next twelve months.
- By June 30, I will identify and investigate three prison or drug rehabilitation programs and join one.

Giving

Definition: People with the gift of giving are super-givers who share material resources generously and cheerfully with those in need. They have a special ability to detect the material needs of others and feel a strong impulse to give without any self-doubt afterwards. They are thrifty, resourceful, and money-wise. They make wise decisions to earn money, motivated by the desire to give more to others, often anonymously.

Examples: Anonymously gives significant amounts as a percentage of their resources to people and ministries in need.

SMART Goal Examples:

- By June 30, I will ask the church if I can help one person who has a financial need and will write a check to satisfy that need.
- By June 30, I will select one special need of a missionary that I can entirely fulfill and write a check to pay for it.
- By June 30, I will increase my giving to the church by 20 percent.

Leadership

Definition: People with the gift of leadership can plan, organize, supervise, and motivate a group of people to accomplish a common goal in a relationship-oriented rather than task-oriented manner. They see the big picture of a project, break it down into a series of subtasks, delegate the tasks to others, and motivate the group to accomplish the project.

Examples: Leads a church's evangelistic outreach by planning the event; scheduling speakers; and coordinating, supervising, and motivating volunteers.

SMART Goal Examples:

- By June 30, I will inquire at church to see if there are any projects that need leaders.
- By June 30, I will develop a ministry proposal for the church, breaking down a project into a series of tasks and due dates, and share the idea with church leaders or friends to confirm the project's need and feasibility.
- By June 30, I will make a list of six ministry organizations, contact each one to inquire if they need a project leader, select one, and volunteer.

Mercy

Definition: People with the gift of mercy offer compassion and encouragement to people who are suffering. Mercy givers are people persons who readily form relationships with others, are gentle and tenderhearted, can extend unconditional love to others, and are attentive to the distress in others, feeling compelled to ease their pain.

Examples: Performs work as a chaplain, counseling people involved in tragedy; visits shut-ins; volunteers for funerals at church; ministers to the poor.

SMART Goal Examples:

- By June 30, I will volunteer with the caring ministry at my church and visit hospitals or shut-ins.
- By June 30, I will make a list of six caring ministries, such as the Salvation Army and Stephen Ministry, research them, and volunteer for one.
- By June 30, I will make a list of facilities, such as nursing homes, prisons, hospitals, and food shelves, within a radius of ten miles of my home, choose one, and volunteer.

Contact your church to see if it offers a test to determine which spiritual gifts the Holy Spirit has given to you. Alternatively, you can take online spiritual gift tests. First google "spiritual gift test" or "spiritual gift inventory." You will find tests such as this: https://www.freeshapetest.com/. Please note that spiritual gift tests are not foolproof, so you may wish to confirm your results with family and friends.

Utilizing your spiritual gifts in a ministry to serve the church and advance God's kingdom is immensely satisfying and will earn rewards in heaven. The key is to start. Once you are active and develop your spiritual gift, God will increase your capacity and lead you to greater responsibility. He may open doors to new ministry opportunities or may bestow another spiritual gift to you.

It's easier to turn a heavy object in motion than at rest. So it is with employing our spiritual gifts. Just get started. Once we've started, God will direct us to the ministry that can employ our spiritual gift.

We are responsible for using our spiritual gifts or losing them and the rewards they can earn (Matthew 25:14–30). There can be no greater joy and purpose in life than to use our spiritual gift, help the needy, and work on a team to fulfill the Great Commission. However, progress in life is not a straight line, and setbacks can occur. Therefore, when we encounter frustration or pain, we must hold fast to and stand on God's promises, which is the subject of the next chapter.

8

Standing on the Promises of God

Life does not follow a level or straight path. It weaves in and out and lurches up and down. Sometimes the path is blocked. Sometimes it seems to be completely washed out. Sometimes it climbs steeply and is exhausting, then plummets and is scary. The path of life is uneven, and to reach our destination, we must keep our eyes on the prize.

> Since, then, you have been raised with Christ, set your hearts on things above, where Christ is, seated at the right hand of God. (Colossians 3:1)

Sometimes our objective is simply to persevere, as the writer of Hebrews reminds us:

> You need to persevere so that when you have done the will of God, you will receive what he has promised. (Hebrews 10:36)

To persevere, we must claim the promises of God that are provided to those who have accepted Jesus Christ as Lord and Savior. We have identified twelve promises to claim that we have placed within five categories:

1. Eternal life
2. Members of a royal family
3. Where we will live when we die
4. What we will do when we die
5. Rewards we will receive when we die

We will later contrast the promises for believers with promises for unbelievers.

Promises for Believers

1. Eternal Life

Eternal life. Most importantly, God promises us eternal life in heaven if we place our faith in Christ. If we believe that Jesus Christ died as payment for our sins through God's graciousness and that nothing else will grant us admission to heaven, we will receive eternal life.

> For God so loved the world that he gave his one and only Son, that whoever believes in him shall not perish but have eternal life. (John 3:16)

No more sorrow. This eternal life will contain no death, grief, or pain.

> He will wipe every tear from their eyes. There will be no more death or mourning or crying or pain, for the old order of things has passed away. (Revelation 21:4)

Glorified bodies. We will have glorified bodies, like the resurrected Jesus. The physical laws of the material world will not constrain us. We will travel to destinations instantly, unconstrained by distance, and appear and disappear at will, unconstrained by doors and walls.

> Who, by the power that enables him to bring everything under his control, will transform our lowly bodies so that they will be like his glorious body. (Philippians 3:21)

> It is sown a natural body, it is raised a spiritual body. If there is a natural body, there is also a spiritual body. (1 Corinthians 15:44)

2. Members of a Royal Family

Member of royal family. When born again, we are admitted to an exclusive family, with saints as brothers and sisters and the God of the universe as our Father. We are God's children. Consider how human mothers and fathers love their children. How much more so does God love us! We can even call God "Dad" or "Daddy."

> Because you are his sons, God sent the Spirit of his Son into our hearts, the Spirit who calls out, "*Abba*, Father."
> (Galatians 4:6)

Heirs to a fortune. As a child of God, we are also an heir of His. This is better than being an heir of Jeff Bezos or Bill Gates. We are God's heir. In a place without sin, God can lavish gifts on us, such as mansions and clothes, without the unintended consequences of jealousy or overindulgence. God has unlimited resources. Bezos and Gates do not.

> So you are no longer a slave, but God's child; and since you are his child, God has made you also an heir.
> (Galatians 4:7)

Guaranteed inheritance. This inheritance is guaranteed. There is no chance we will get written out of the will.

> Praise be to the God and Father of our Lord Jesus Christ! In his great mercy he has given us new birth into a living hope through the resurrection of Jesus Christ from the dead, and into an inheritance that can never perish, spoil or fade. This inheritance is kept in heaven for you. (1 Peter 1:3–4)

Guaranteed arrival. We can't make a mistake that will cancel our ticket to heaven. The Holy Spirit seals us and guarantees our arrival. It's not next-day service; it's instant service. That is blessed assurance.

> And you also were included in Christ when you heard the message of truth, the gospel of your salvation. When you believed, you were marked in him with a seal, the promised Holy Spirit, who is a deposit guaranteeing

our inheritance until the redemption of those who are God's possession—to the praise of his glory. (Ephesians 1:13–14)

Living with God. Imagine having a bodyguard and the comfort that would convey. Well, imagine living with the God of the universe Himself! Nothing to fear. Nothing to make us feel unwelcome or unimportant or unworthy.

And I heard a loud voice from the throne saying, "Look! God's dwelling place is now among the people, and he will dwell with them. They will be his people, and God himself will be with them and be their God." (Revelation 21:3)

3. Where Believers Will Live When They Die

Mansions. We can look forward to living in mansions as the King James Version describes below. Just think of living in a mansion like one found at mansionsglobal.com. Money is no object to God.

In my Father's house are many mansions: if it were not so, I would have told you. I go to prepare a place for you. (John 14:2)

New Jerusalem. If you like the allure of big, glittering cities, you will absolutely love the New Jerusalem, a city of pure translucent gold, lit by the glory of God.

The wall was made of jasper, and the city of pure gold, as pure as glass. (Revelation 21:18)

There will be no more night. They will not need the light of a lamp or the light of the sun, for the Lord God will give them light. And they will reign for ever and ever. (Revelation 22:5)

4. What Believers Will Do When They Die .

Rulers and priests. We will be rulers and priests serving the Lord with responsibilities in proportion to the crowns we earn. God will fully equip us to do our jobs, and there will be no job burnout.

> "You have made them to be a kingdom and priests
> to serve our God, and they will reign on the earth."
> (Revelation 5:10)

5. Rewards Believers Will Receive When They Die

Rewards. The Christian life, pursued in obedience to God's Word, and with His glorification as the object, will accrue rewards in heaven. God has unlimited resources and creativity, so these rewards will excite us more than a child receiving a scooter or iPod at Christmas.

> "Do not store up for yourselves treasures on earth,
> where moths and vermin destroy, and where thieves
> break in and steal. But store up for yourselves treasures
> in heaven, where moths and vermin do not destroy, and
> where thieves do not break in and steal. For where your
> treasure is, there your heart will be also." (Matthew
> 6:19–21)

Promises for Unbelievers

Quite a different set of promises exist for those who do *not* believe in Jesus or trust in His death and resurrection to pay for their sins. These promises are chilling.

1. Eternal Life

Eternal life. People whose names are not in the Book of Life, who have not placed their trust in the atoning sacrifice of Jesus, receive eternal life as well. Only, that life will be spent in the Lake of Fire.

> Anyone whose name was not found written in the book of life was thrown into the lake of fire. (Revelation 20:15)

Much more sorrow. For unbelievers, eternal life will be one long feeling of regret and sorrow for rejecting Jesus as Savior and Lord. They will gnash their teeth, realizing that the Bible was true. They had a chance to accept the truth of the Bible, but they foolishly rejected it.

> This is how it will be at the end of the age. The angels will come and separate the wicked from the righteous and throw them into the blazing furnace, where there will be weeping and gnashing of teeth. (Matthew 13:49-50)

Broken-down bodies. For unbelievers, there will be torment in hell. Their bodies will be a source of reproach, pain, and discomfort.

> Do not be afraid of those who kill the body but cannot kill the soul. Rather, be afraid of the One who can destroy both soul and body in hell. (Matthew 10:28)

2. Members of a Wicked Family

Member of a wicked family. Rather than living with a loving God, unbelievers in hell will live with Satan, his demons, and those who practiced the worst sort of wickedness on earth.

> But the cowardly, the unbelieving, the vile, the murderers, the sexually immoral, those who practice magic arts, the idolaters and all liars—they will be consigned to the fiery lake of burning sulfur. This is the second death. (Revelation 21:8)

Heirs to torment. The account of the rich man in hell told by Jesus illustrates that earthly riches do not cross over into the afterlife. The rich man's fortune on earth was all he was going to receive. After death, there was no fortune waiting for him, only torment. In contrast, the poor beggar in life received riches after death because he believed in God and the promised Messiah.

> In Hades, where he was in torment, he looked up and saw Abraham far away, with Lazarus by his side. (Luke 16:23)

Guaranteed punishment. The only inheritance for unbelievers in hell is torment in unquenchable fire. Not the extreme pain of burning alive but a lasting heat that dries and never relents. (The account that Jesus tells in Luke 16:19–31, about a rich man in hell, indicates that the person in hell is not literally burning alive. If that were the case, the person would not be carrying on a conversation. There is agonizing heat and dryness though, because the rich man requests water to cool his tongue.)

> His winnowing fork is in his hand, and he will clear his threshing floor, gathering his wheat into the barn and burning up the chaff with unquenchable fire. (Matthew 3:12)

Guaranteed arrival. Those who do not believe in Jesus also face a guaranteed arrival at a destination. Only it's not heaven; it's hell. Jesus addresses hell more than any other topic (e.g., Matthew 10:28, 13:42, 25:30; Mark 9:43, 48; Luke 16:19–31).

> "Not everyone who says to me, 'Lord, Lord,' will enter the kingdom of heaven, but only the one who does the will of my Father who is in heaven. Many will say to me on that day, 'Lord, Lord, did we not prophesy in your name and in your name drive out demons and in your name perform many miracles?' Then I will tell them plainly, 'I never knew you. Away from me, you evildoers!'" (Matthew 7:21–23)

Separated from God. Unbelievers in hell will live apart from God and His glorious majesty and kingdom. They lived apart from God on earth, and that is their choice in death.

> They will be punished with everlasting destruction and shut out from the presence of the Lord and from the glory of his might. (2 Thessalonians 1:9)

3. Where Unbelievers Will Live When They Die

Darkness. Unbelievers in hell will have no brightly lit mansions awaiting them. Rather, they will be out in the darkness, separated from God, where they will gnash their teeth with regret.

> But the subjects of the kingdom will be thrown outside, into the darkness, where there will be weeping and gnashing of teeth. (Matthew 8:12)

Unquenchable fire. No glittering city awaits unbelievers in hell. Just unquenchable heat and feasting worms.

> And if your eye causes you to stumble, pluck it out. It is better for you to enter the kingdom of God with one eye than to have two eyes and be thrown into hell, where the worms that eat them do not die, and the fire is not quenched. (Mark 9:47–48)

4. What Unbelievers Will Do When They Die

Mourners and regretters. There will be no useful work in hell. Time will pass by with unbelievers mourning past bad decisions and sin and regretting that they had a chance to accept Jesus as Savior and Lord and rejected Him.

> The Son of Man will send out his angels, and they will weed out of his kingdom everything that causes sin and all who do evil. They will throw them into the blazing

furnace, where there will be weeping and gnashing of teeth. (Matthew 13:41–42)

5. Punishment Unbelievers Will Receive When They Die

Punishment. Hell is everlasting torment for rejecting Jesus and accepting anything in His place, particularly idols or Satan, and for becoming so depraved that one pursues and promotes sinful practices with relish.

> And the smoke of their torment will rise for ever and ever. There will be no rest day or night for those who worship the beast and its image, or for anyone who receives the mark of its name. (Revelation 14:11)

As you can see, there couldn't be a greater contrast between the promises given to believers and those given to unbelievers. For those people who repent of their sins and trust in Jesus alone to pay for their sins, there are wonderful promises in store for them in heaven. For those who turn from God and His Son, there is the promise of torment.

Conclusion

We have answered the most important question in your life: where you go when you die. There is a heaven and hell. There is a holy God with whom you can spend eternity. However, humans are sinful and incompatible with God's holiness. We are contaminated with the sin virus and cannot disinfect ourselves. Nevertheless, God has clearly provided a way for us to reach heaven and live with Him. He has paid the way for us by sacrificing Himself on the cross for our sins through Jesus Christ. All we must do is believe and humbly accept that payment.

We have described the amazing prophecies fulfilled in the Bible and the prophetic timeline for the future. We have specified worthy goals that will earn crowns and rewards in heaven and have explained how to earn those crowns and rewards on earth. You must serve God, live a life pleasing to God, and pursue ministries that employ your spiritual gifts. We have also provided a way to keep your focus fixed on your goals by standing on the promises of God when you encounter obstacles.

The choice is obvious. Turn from a life of sin and accept Jesus as your Lord and Savior. From that point, you will earn rewards and be awarded crowns and responsibilities in heaven. Start earning today. Find your spiritual gift(s), create SMART goals, and get going. God will direct you to a worthwhile ministry that will provide immense satisfaction here on earth and assurance that you are serving the living God and earning treasure in heaven.

To our God and Father be glory for ever and ever. Amen.

—Philippians 4:20

Plan of Salvation

Good News

- Men and women are sinners—we are born into sin.
- God the Father cannot tolerate sin.
- But God loves you and wants you to be with Him in heaven.
- God sent His only Son, Jesus, to pay the debt for your sins.
- Only Jesus, who is God, can pay this debt.
- He died on the cross for your sins.
- He rose from the dead three days later.
- You need to repent of your sins and trust in Jesus as your Savior.

God loves you so much that He gave His only Son, Jesus Christ, to die for your sins. If you believe in Him, turn from your sins, and make Jesus the Lord of your life, you will have eternal life with Him in Heaven.

Will You Pray This Prayer Today?

Dear God,

I know I'm a sinner, and I ask for your forgiveness. I believe Jesus Christ is Your Son. I believe that He died for my sin and that you raised Him to life. I want to trust Him as my Savior and follow Him as Lord, from this day forward. Guide my life and help me to do your will. I pray this in the name of Jesus. Amen.

_____   _____
           Date   Signature

If you have prayed this prayer and accepted Jesus Christ into your life by faith, please contact us at TrainingGuideMinistry.com

Endnotes

1 Murphy, Caryle, "Most Americans believe in heaven … and hell," Pew Research Center, November 10, 2015, accessed December 24 2016, https://www.pewresearch. org/fact-tank/2015/11/10/most-americans-believe-in-heaven-and-hell/.

2 Ballard, Jamie, "45% of Americans believe that ghosts and demons exist," YouGov, October 21, 2019, accessed December 24, 2019, https://today.yougov.com/topics/lifestyle/articles-reports/2019/10/21/ paranormal-beliefs-ghosts-demons-poll.

3 Barna, "Most Americans Believe in Supernatural Healing," Barna, September 29, 2016, accessed December 24, 2019, https://www.barna.com/research/ americans-believe-supernatural-healing/.

4 Billy Graham Evangelistic Association, "The Glory of Christ: 5 Ways Jesus Proved He's the Messiah," Billy Graham Evangelistic Association, December 24, 2015, accessed May 25, 2020, https://billygraham.org/story/ the-glory-of-christ-5-ways-jesus-proved-hes-the-messiah/.

5 CBN, "Biblical Prophecies Fulfilled by Jesus," CBN, accessed December 26, 2019, https://www1.cbn.com/biblestudy/biblical-prophecies-fulfilled-by-jesus.

6 McDowell, Josh, *The New Evidence That Demands a Verdict*, Nashville: Thomas Nelson Publishers, 1999.

7 Alcorn, Randy, *Heaven*, Carol Stream, IL: Tyndale House Publishers, Inc., 2004, 259.

8 Garlow, James and Wall, Keith, *Heaven and the Afterlife*, Minneapolis: Bethany House Publishers, 2009, 157.

9 Robinson, Rich, "First Fruits in the Bible: What Does it Have to Do with Resurrection from the Dead?," Jews for Jesus, March 1, 1997, accessed January 1, 2020, https://jewsforjesus.org/publications/newsletter/ newsletter-mar-1997/first-fruits-in-the-bible-what-does-it-have-to-do-with-resurrection-from-the-dead/.

10 Sproul, R. C., *The Holiness of God*, Wheaton, IL: Tyndale House Publishers, Inc., 1998, 26.

11 Banks, Adelle, "Hymn society tournament reveals 'greatest hymn of all time'," Religion News Service, July 19, 2019, accessed January 20, 2020, https://religionnews. com/2019/07/19/hymn-society-tournament-reveals-greatest-hymn-of-all-time/.

12 Samaritan's Purse, "Knowing God," Samaritan's Purse, accessed January 20, 2020, https://www.samaritanspurse.org/our-ministry/knowing-god/.

13 Frantzman, Seth, "Fallout from the Turkey-Iran-Russia meeting," The Jerusalem Post, April 6, 2018, accessed March 4, 2020, https://www.jpost.com/International/Fallout-from-the-Turkey-Iran-Russia-meeting-549022.

14 Sharon, Jeremy, "Temple-ready altar dedicated on last day of Hanukkah by activist groups," The Jerusalem Post, December 10, 2018, accessed January 16, 2020, https://www.jpost.com/Israel-News/Temple-ready-altar-dedicated-on-last-day-of-Hanukkah-by-activist-groups-573980.

15 Berkowitz, Adam, "Red Heifer Birth, Paves Way for Renewed Temple Service," Israel365 News, September 5, 2018, accessed December 3, 2020, https://www.israel365news.com/113476/temple-institute-certifies-red-heifer/.

16 Bas-Wohlert, Camille "Microchips get under the skin of technophile Swedes," Phys.org, May 13, 2018, accessed January 16, 2020, https://phys.org/news/2018-05-microchips-skin-technophile-swedes.html.

17 Alliance Defending Freedom, "Masterpiece Cakeshop v. Colorado Civil Rights Commission," Alliance Defending Freedom, accessed January 9, 2020, https://adflegal.org/detailspages/case-details/masterpiece-cakeshop-v.-craig.

18 Alliance Defending Freedom, "Barronelle Stutzman," Alliance Defending Freedom, accessed January 9, 2020, https://adflegal.org/detailspages/client-stories-details/barronelle-stutzman.

19 Lowry, Lindy, "In Egypt, Families of 21 Martyrs Beheaded by ISIS Feel 'Inner Peace' After Remains Returned," Open Doors, May 16, 2018, accessed January 9, 2020, available: https://www.opendoorsusa.org/christian-persecution/stories/in-egypt-families-of-21-martyrs-beheaded-by-isis-feel-inner-peace-after-remains-returned/.

20 Alcorn, Heaven, 217–224.

21 Alcorn, Heaven, 225–235.

22 Stanley, Charles. F., Ministering Through Spiritual Gifts, Nashville, TN: Thomas Nelson, Inc., 2010.

23 MacArther, John, "Spiritual Gifts," Grace to You, accessed January 22, 2021, available: https://www.gty.org/library/study-guides/100/spiritual-gifts.

Index

About the Authors

David L. Johnson is a former college teacher with a PhD in education. He has served for many years in a prison ministry, is a certified chaplain, and is a member of a large nondenominational evangelical church in the Twin Cities, Minnesota.

Richard A. Hansen is a retired commercial airline pilot. He has served for many years in a prison ministry and a nursing home ministry, is a licensed chaplain, and is also a member of the same church in the Twin Cities.

Contact Us

By mail:

> Training Guide Ministry
> P.O. Box 533
> Shakopee, MN 55379

Online:

> TrainingGuideMinistry.com
> Info@TrainingGuideMinistry.com

Further Your Study of This Book

STUDY GUIDE

This is the 129-page companion study guide for *Training Guide for Heaven: Running for the Prize*. There is a lesson in the study guide for each chapter of the book. Each lesson provides key points at a glance, application discussion questions for each key point, a going deeper question, and a quiz with answers.